Contents

Part 1: Welcome to Post Compulsory Education (PCE)   1

  1 Introduction   2

  2 What is Post Compulsory Education?   7

  3 Teaching and learning starting points   17

Part 2: Don't panic   27

  4 Meeting the initial challenges   28

  5 Access for all – working with Skills for Life   41

  6 The 14–19 curriculum   48

  7 Information skills, or 'if you can't find it yourself, how do you expect   55
      your students to?'

  8 Positive strategies for managing change   60

  9 Mentoring matters   65

Part 3: Surviving in the classroom   73

  10 Developing your specialist subject   74

  11 Working with a diverse student body   80

  12 Managing challenging behaviour   89

  13 Putting the 'learning' into e-learning   97

Part 4: Surviving outside the classroom   105

  14 Working with colleagues   106

  15 Working under pressure and managing conflict   114

  16 Are you teaching in a learning organisation?   123

Part 5: Moving out of the deep end   131

  17 Reality check . . . how's it going?   132

  18 Dealing with bureaucracy and inspection   141

  19 Managing your managers   148

Part 6: Moving towards mastery   155
20   Developing leadership skills   156
21   Becoming a reflective professional   165
22   You can get involved in research and professional development   172
23   Future gazing – where and what next?   181

Glossary   188

In at the Deep End

A Survival Guide for Teachers in Post Compulsory Education

JIM CRAWLEY

 David Fulton Publishers

David Fulton Publishers Ltd
The Chiswick Centre, 414 Chiswick High Road, London W4 5TF

www.fultonpublishers.co.uk
www.onestopeducation.co.uk

David Fulton Publishers is a division of Granada Learning Limited, part of ITV plc.

British Library Cataloguing in Publication Data
A catalogue record for this book is available from the British Library.

ISBN: 1 84312 253 7

First published 2005 by David Fulton Publishers, reprinted 2005
10 9 8 7 6 5 4 3 2

Typeset by Servis Filmsetting Ltd, Longsight, Manchester
Printed and bound in Great Britain

To Jan, my beautiful and wise wife, and Dan, Tim and Rosi, my children from somewhere near heaven.

As this is my first book, I need to thank Dad for some important parts of the creative spark, Mum for the range of emotions to go with it, my identical twin brother John for being both very similar to and very different from me, and my sister Sue for providing the balance that a male twin needs from his sister, John's wife Helen and Sue's husband Cader for being the nicest sister-in-law and brother-in-law it's possible to be, and my young beautiful nieces Isabella and Olivia, and older but just as nice niece Sara and nephew Rechad.

Be sure that the rest of the sentences in this book won't be as long as this one!

Acknowledgements

Thanks to my readers Chris Hill, Carol Minchington and Caroline Harvey, who, at the time of writing, are all still working at 'the chalk face' (although chalk has long since disappeared – is there a 'board pen face'?). They have all needed considerable survival skills themselves over their many years of experience in PCE.

Special thanks to my wife Jan, who doesn't work in education, but being wise, and working in community development, has offered a perspective from outside the system, which has been invaluable. She has also been brave enough to tell me what she really thinks about the book, which I think has made it much better than it might have been.

Thanks also to my editor, Tracey Alcock, who has so enthusiastically supported the concept and writing of the book that I hope it may be a real contribution to help teachers in the 'Cinderella sector'.

The support and feedback from them all has helped to produce a book which I'm very proud of.

Preface

In many ways, this is the book I've been learning to write for 30 years.

In 1975, after an unsuccessful attempt to get into a job connected with TV, I took on some part-time work in three youth clubs in Bristol, using video to work with what would now be called 'disaffected youths'. This turned out to be really enjoyable, both for me and (as far as I could tell) for them, and we made some good little videos (using two suitcases full of equipment which would now fit into your pocket). What also happened was that the youngsters who took part grew noticeably in confidence and obviously learnt some new skills. I seemed to be reasonably able to help motivate them and to work out activities and tasks which would get their interest and keep them going, and I really wanted to do more of this. Although I didn't realise it at the time, this was my introduction to teaching in Post Compulsory Education (PCE), and that's where I've been ever since!

I've worked in two further education (FE) colleges for most of my working life in PCE and have been involved in adult education, general education, vocational education and work-based learning, all from the base of an FE college. I've now finally arrived in the (slightly) calmer waters of higher education. The work has included teaching almost every type of group you can imagine (and possibly some you'd rather not!). I've taught literacy and social skills to unemployed young adults; history to adults on Access to Higher Education courses; interview techniques to adults on work preparation courses; GCSE computer studies to 18-year-olds (teaching I was given just because I owned my own Sinclair Spectrum!); and even general studies to apprentices in the graveyard 5–6 pm shift. Now I supervise Master of Arts students. I have taught approximately 1,000 teachers working in PCE either for their full teaching qualification or on the shorter, introductory courses such as the Stage One. My non-teaching roles and responsibilities have included organising adult education, managing higher education courses and managing a continuing education department which changed its name about every four years, in a further education college which changed its principal almost as often.

Over that time, much has changed beyond all recognition, and yet some things have remained strangely the same. PCE has always sat somewhat uncomfortably between school and higher education and exerts less power and influence. In fact it appears to often exert virtually no power or influence at all. PCE has always worked with disadvantaged members of the community, and readily embraced diversity among its students and staff. In all honesty, the last 10–15 years I worked in a college saw the working situation for teachers and other staff deteriorate into what can only be described as thinly veiled chaos. On an ongoing basis at the moment, managerialism dominates, inspection terrifies and the curriculum changes and reshapes itself like some kind of endlessly morphing alien. It sometimes seems more like a cunning plan to keep us all under control by ensuring we are so absurdly busy that rebellion is out of the question (we're all far too tired and run down!). Most of us still like to believe that we are trying to make the world a better place, but at times that can feel like a rather distant prospect.

There is one thing which keeps us all going, even in darker times. Despite all the changes, reorganisations and initiatives, when we get into what we call our classrooms with our students, what goes on essentially stays the same. As a teacher, or as one of a team of teachers, we work really hard to help our students to learn, and many of them actually do.

Many people describe PCE as a sector which is complicated, difficult to define and equally difficult to develop as a coherent entity, and I'm not going to disagree with that. What does however bind the sector in the most meaningful way is the shared enterprise of all the teachers who are working together to improve the life chances of their students.

In reading this book, you'll quickly see how positive about PCE it is. If you cut me in half, I think you'd see 'education for all' written inside, like a seaside rock. I hope the book will:

- encourage teachers in PCE to feel part of a shared and valued community;
- help a few teachers to do their job better, and enjoy it more;
- help more members of the community to learn new things.

If it does, it will have been well worth writing.

Who is this book for?

The main audience will be teachers new to PCE, probably in the early stages of their careers (perhaps the first two years). A significant proportion will be working towards completing their initial teacher training during those first years. This book will provide both practical support and guidance for their day-to-day teaching, and strategies, activities and space to reflect which will be useful on courses such as the Certificate of Education. It will however also have relevance for all staff teaching and supporting learning (whether they are new or experienced) in the growing Post Compulsory Education sector, which now encompasses further education, a range of 14–19 provision, adult and community learning, workplace learning and a significant amount of higher education.

Many of the themes and topics are universal to all teachers, so it should also be helpful if you are teaching in a school.

The book takes an approach to content which is consciously eclectic, as there are many ideas, models, activities and examples out there which can be useful for teachers in PCE. It unashamedly draws on many, not all of which necessarily agree with each other. Theory and academic thinking are not forgotten and are drawn in to support the development of practice and to make that practice more meaningful. All of the content is focused on the book's central objective, which is to help you survive and develop as an effective, confident, committed and reflective teacher. The influences and ideas therefore may to some degree be mixed, but the message remains the same. That message is that teaching is an exceptionally important profession and that doing it well is a goal we should all strive for together.

Much of what is in the book will also give managers in PCE a clearer insight into what their teaching staff really experience on a day-to-day basis and how they try to manage some of the pressures they are under. It would be a practical and straightforward way for a manager to get into the world of the teacher and could be a real help for managers who genuinely want to support their staff, improve quality and get better results!

If you enjoy the book, take a look at my web site, 'Itslife', which is intended to provide information and links to other web sites for those who are working in PCE.

You can find it at

http://www.itslifejimbutnotasweknowit.org.uk

PART 1

Welcome to Post Compulsory Education (PCE)

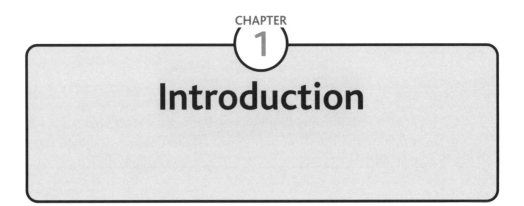

Introduction

To start in the way we mean to continue, this chapter will introduce the upbeat and positive rationale behind the book, which is essentially that teaching in the post compulsory sector, although at times challenging, exhausting and frustrating, is also often a hugely enjoyable and rewarding area of work, which makes a contribution like no other to civil society. Guidance on how the book can work for you best and how it is structured to provide variety and activity is also included, and something of a 'call to arms' to send you all on your way looking forward to your teaching and of course to the rest of the book.

An introduction to the deep end

As a teacher you bring your unique life experience, personality and skills with you to the job of teaching and you will often need to draw deeply on them in the rich and varied world which is PCE. In addition to preparing and carrying out your teaching in a rapidly changing and developing curriculum you will encounter a maze of bureaucracy and administration. While you are trying to prepare for inspection, working towards the latest quality standard or benchmark, and expecting your next internal classroom observation, there are some essential personal qualities which will keep you going and help you survive as a working professional. They are enthusiasm, energy, resourcefulness and resilience, and perhaps the most indispensable of all, and at times the single most important, a sense of humour! If you don't possess most of these qualities in abundance at the start of your teaching career, you may want to take a careful breath and consider a more peaceful life. Believe me, there will be times when laughing is the only possible reaction to some of the situations you will encounter.

Starting work as a teacher can be complicated and confusing, as there is much to learn and never enough time to learn it. Many of the 'official' parts of being a new teacher can seem almost irrelevant as you struggle to plan and organise your next teaching week of more than 20 hours of teaching. It can feel very much like being in at the deep end and at times sinking could be much more straightforward than swimming.

There are however many things which can help over the early stages of being a teacher, including assistance from colleagues, support from the culture and habits of your organisation, and learning through your successes and mistakes. The trouble is that by the time you have learnt all these things, you have often already been teaching for one or two years. Then of course they all change again. You will have thought often 'If only I'd known that when I started.' This book has used the benefits of a considerable pool of experience of the author and many friends and teaching colleagues to try to provide you with some of those answers, hints and tips in advance, or at least earlier than you would get them if you relied on just learning from your own experience.

As we will explore in more detail later in the book,

learning is something essential in human life.

Foley (2004), when discussing adult learning, puts this nicely

As . . . David Kolb (1984) has noted, learning is human beings' primary mode of adaptation: if we don't learn, we may not survive, and we certainly don't prosper . . . All human activity has a learning dimension. People learn informally and formally, in many different settings; in workplaces, in families, through leisure activities, through community activities, and in political action.   (Foley 2004: 4)

Although this comment is about adult learning, and PCE works with students as young as 14, it resonates strongly within the overall approach of this book. Even though the implication from such a view is that teachers and teaching are a relatively small part of the wide world of learning, it is a crucial part, which in many cases and situations can be the key to positive and successful learning.

At the heart of this book is therefore one of the most positive aspirations which any career can possibly have. As you strive to combine the 'essential you' and those other qualities with important skills, understandings and approaches relating to teaching and learning, you genuinely are on one of life's most important, yet often underrated missions, which is to help other people to learn.

You may or may not feel that education can change the world, but there is no doubt that at some stage, and if you're both lucky and good at your job, you will often help to change someone else's world and life for the better.

Never underestimate the power of learning.

As a teacher, what will drive you on is the knowledge that learning can still transform and can really make a difference. Let's face it, if that isn't worth trying to do as well as you can, what is?

Good luck with the journey!

Making the book work for you

There is an intentional progression through the book, which shadows the journey of the teachers reading it. In the early chapters you will cover topics and themes which will be most relevant to new teachers, at the time when they feel immersed in the 'deep end'. We will then progress to more detail about areas of work which you will take on as you gain more experience and the latter sections focus on the anticipated development of a more confident mastery of the craft of teaching. The structure is designed to help your career pathway to move in the same direction. Navigation through the book is clear and straightforward with generally short chapters, each of which starts with a summary of content. Themes covered include:

- basic principles and practicalities of teaching and learning;
- management and survival skills which will help your day-to-day work;
- developing support networks;
- extending your specialist subject;
- working with learning technology;
- getting the best from mentoring;
- being 'actively critical';
- managing your managers.

A glossary of relevant terms appears in the appendices, while a bibliography is included on a chapter-by-chapter basis. Use is not made of learning objectives or detailed mapping to national standards, partly because national standards for PCE are undergoing a period of change at present, but mainly because this book is much more concerned with accessibility and a developmental approach than closely mapping to particular standards. Much of the content will however map across to teaching standards in terms of topics, professional knowledge, values and the actual skills involved, but it is a more holistic notion of teaching which underpins the whole book, as will be evident from the start.

National standards do have some benefits however, and defining some areas of teaching effectively is one of them. The Further Education National Training Organisation (FENTO) published national standards for further education teachers in January 1999, and although at the time of writing they are being extended and rewritten for the newly extended PCE sector, which is much bigger than further education, they do contain a helpful starting point for us all. According to those FENTO standards, the 'key purpose' for a teacher is 'to provide high-quality teaching, to create effective opportunities for learning and to enable all students to achieve to the best of their ability' (FENTO 1999: 3). There is little wrong with that as a definition of what a teacher's main working rationale is, but we will take a fresh approach to that key purpose through the subject matter of this book.

Thinking Points and Strategies for Survival

A new feature for a book of this kind is the use of 'Thinking Points'. These provide focused, accessible and realistic activities, examples, scenarios and reflections, or 'mini tasks', which create variety and something of a pause for thought and reflection. They may take the reader away from the text to think about or do something directly related to their practice, or provide a chance to try out something new and reflect on it before moving on to the next section or chapter. They are also activities which can be adapted for use in a wide range of teaching situations, so will hopefully provide you with ready-made teaching resources.

Food for thought is interesting, but won't help you survive on its own, so I also suggest ways you could act on your reflections. 'Strategies for Survival' will therefore often follow Thinking Points, so that you can make use of them on the journey out of the deep end.

The index

The index to the book is organised to ensure you can find content easily on key topics such as learning, planning and supporting students, and will provide a different route through the book if that suits you better.

The vision

What can often seem like a fragmented, poor quality, badly managed and indeed chaotic sector actually achieves amazing results for and with many of its students. This is often despite circumstances which are as difficult and challenging as you could possibly imagine for the students. The people who are at the heart of the many successes in PCE are of course the students themselves, but the key professionals, who more than anyone else deserve a share of that success, are the teachers. This book is intended to help teachers in PCE extend that success into the future and help the sector to get the recognition it deserves.

References

Foley, G. (ed.) (2004) *Dimensions of Learning. Adult Education and Training in a Global Era.* Maidenhead: Open University Press

Further Education National Training Organisation (1999) *Standards for Teaching and Supporting Learning in Further Education in England and Wales.* London: FENTO

Kolb, D. (1984) *Experiential Learning: Experience as the Source of Learning and Development.* Englewood Cliffs, New Jersey: Prentice-Hall

What is Post Compulsory Education?

Teaching takes place in a rapidly changing world and this chapter introduces that context of rapid change in the world outside and shows you how as teachers you can positively encounter and manage that change as part of your work. A description of just what is meant by Post Compulsory Education in this book follows, with examples of the kind of teaching situations you may find yourself encountering. The chapter closes by outlining the diversity of the student body in PCE, by which time you should have a deeper understanding of the nature of the sector and aspects of your teaching role within it.

The changing world of Post Compulsory Education

Life in the twenty-first century will be fascinating if the range of changes which took place during the latter stages of the twentieth century continues at the same rate, as all indicators suggest it will.

Just reflect on these momentous late twentieth-century events:

- the Berlin Wall was torn down in 1989, with the subsequent collapse of the Soviet Union;
- Nelson Mandela was released from prison in 1990 and Apartheid in South Africa ended;
- mobile phones as we know them now did not exist in 1980, but by 2003 in the UK alone there were 50.2 million subscribers (MOA 2003);
- the first email program was used in 1972 and 950 million Internet users are forecast across the world by December 2006 (IDATE 2003).

With many social, technological, political and economic changes taking place around the world, it would be somewhat odd not to see this reflected in the world of education in general, and in PCE in particular. The ways in which this climate of change can affect you as a teacher are however both direct and indirect.

Direct change

Direct change affects you in the immediate world of your subject, teaching and students. It can include finding out that the course you have just started getting used to after your first year is changing so significantly in the second year that you are almost starting again from scratch. The introduction of new modules, assessment tasks, verification procedures or completely new areas of the curriculum happens just months (or sometimes even weeks) before your students are due to start and the first teaching sessions due to take place. At the extremes the syllabus or curriculum can change after you have started teaching it.

Piloting anything new is rare to the degree where it is probably best not to expect it. New initiatives, ideas and approaches rain down from government, from your own institution and from the local or regional funding organisation with bewildering frequency. Each one of these is accompanied by another publication, web site or series of staff development events, all combining to produce a mountain of information to digest before real planning can take place. While you are trying to absorb and manage all this direct change, your teaching is probably under the spotlight through internal teaching observations, student evaluation forms or your participation in a teacher training course.

Indirect change

Indirect change is one step removed from the immediate world of your own specialist subject and is often less under your control than direct change. It can be due to new technology, where for example your institutional computer system may be upgraded (not an unusual occurrence), resulting sometimes in a loss of services such as email for a few hours or even days. It's only when you haven't got something that you realise how much you rely on it and email is one of those things. Another example may be when the senior manager running your section or department leaves or moves into a different internal job suddenly (not unusual in PCE). Their replacement may have a very different approach to the person managing you before and your situation could alter dramatically.

One thing you can expect therefore is to be in a rapidly changing world, with what at times can seem like little time to think, let alone to pause, reflect and consider the next step.

This is not to suggest that this much change is a bad thing (although to see some of the people responsible for the changes swap places with us in a reality TV programme and see how they cope with our jobs would be interesting). We would probably all agree that change is certainly challenging, can be unsettling and can be at times veritably unnerving.

Change is a fact of life – get used to working with it!

When you take a more positive view of change, things can start to look somewhat different. Charles Handy (1995: 44) argues effectively about change which 'does not have to be forced on us by crisis and calamity' and suggests change can be 'another word for learning'. He suggests that

> Those who are always learning are those who can ride the waves of change and who see a changing world as full of opportunities not damages. They are the ones most likely to be the survivors in a time of discontinuity. They are also the enthusiasts of new ways and forms and ideas.   (Handy 1995: 44)

This book tries to approach the work of a teacher in PCE very much as the 'learning approach to change'.

THINKING POINT

Your own 'change diary'
This activity will help you to reflect on change which you have recently experienced and use that reflection to help you manage future changes.

- Think back over your last four weeks of teaching. If you haven't started teaching yet, try to look forward to what you are expecting over the same time period.

- Create a simple change diary or change time line by briefly recording all the changes you have experienced. (You don't have to do this with linear text. Feel free to represent the changes in whatever way you feel suits you best.)

- Log the effects of the changes and how you feel you have coped with them.

STRATEGY FOR SURVIVAL

Riding the waves of change
Now you've listed all the changes, group them under two headings, firstly into the ones where, as Handy put it, you have been 'riding the waves of change' and secondly those which have 'washed you into the deep end'.

- In the situations where you managed change better, try to pick out just what you did which made that happen.

- Share your tips for managing change with colleagues and get them to share theirs with you.

- Choose one of your more difficult 'deep end' situations; use the same approach to work out what went wrong and how you can 'ride the waves' next time using some of your successful strategies.

- Try to put the improvements into practice as soon afterwards as possible.

Can we define Post Compulsory Education?

If you were trying to provide a map of or guide to Post Compulsory Education you would need to produce a new edition almost every year, as major changes can happen with great regularity. Even as this book is being written, there are significant policies moving forward which will enlarge the sector and indeed redefine it. Two of the most authoritative recent books have highlighted the problems with defining PCE as follows:

> The field is obviously vast, and it is becoming commonplace to talk as if PCE was about any learning that takes place outside compulsory schooling.
>
> (Armitage, Bryant, Dunnill *et al.* 2003: 6)

> The sector has become a catch-all for the increasing areas of provision which fall outside of the compulsory schooling and higher education remit.
>
> (Fawbert (ed.) 2003: 315)

It is possibly more straightforward to ask, what does the sector do or provide? Consider these facts about learning activity in the UK.

Further education

There are almost 470 further education colleges in the UK, ranging from small colleges with a combined full-time and part-time enrolment of about 5,000 each year to huge, multi-site colleges enrolling 35,000 students a year. There are also just over 100 sixth-form colleges, which provide the qualifications and other activities which would form the sixth form of a secondary school but in a separate college which does only that work. National statistics for further education indicate the size and growth of this part of the sector. There were 5.4 million further education students in the UK during the academic year 2001/2, compared with 2.2 million in 1990/1. Four-fifths of these students in 2001/2 were part time, a similar proportion as in 1990/1 (DfES 2003a).

Every FE college will have many learning programmes based at the main college campus, but in addition there will probably be one or more other campuses. These will probably include a number of outreach centres providing information technology courses and other advice and information. Contracts and courses with employers in the local area, involvement in projects, initiatives, research and development will all also feature in the portfolio of most FE colleges. Some still offer adult education courses in their local community and many have moved into e-learning through some kind of online presence. Further education is therefore not some kind of compact, homogenous operation which works in the same way in every location; even within the same college there can be a wide variety of teaching experiences for those working there.

Adult and Community Learning (ACL)

In November 2002 there were 1.42 million enrolments on adult education courses offered by local education authorities, of which two-thirds were on courses which did not lead to qualifications and three-quarters of the students were women (DfES 2003b). If you have ever been to a local adult education class, you will know that they can take place in schools, leisure centres, public buildings, village halls or even outside. There will probably be A-Levels and GCSEs and leisure-based courses such as embroidery and local history, and many others in a variety which will partly be tailored to meet demand locally. So a teacher in ACL may teach the same subject for several centres and may do as little as one or two hours a week for part of the year or work as much as full time.

Workplace learning

This area tends to be split into work-based learning for young people (programmes such as Modern Apprenticeships), where there were in the region of 270,000 participants in 2001/2, and job-related training (on and off the job) in which over 5 million employees were said to have participated 'in the last four weeks' in 2003 (DfES 2003a). Some of these students will also feature in the other statistics, but this is again a sizeable area, which could include anything from a major multinational company employing thousands of staff and providing its own learning centre on site, to a 'micro business' employing about ten people, where all training is done on the job.

14–19 provision

Locating statistics on this fast-growing area of work in PCE is difficult, but there are significant numbers of 14–19-year-olds now studying in FE colleges on either a full-time or part-time basis. The provision tends to be for vocational courses, or shared with schools and sixth-form colleges, and often involves providing a wider choice between 14 and 19, and developing key skills. The teaching of the group could be on a college site, in a shared development between schools and colleges or in a separate specialised centre purpose-built for 14–19 provision.

A definition

All of the above can be found within our definition of PCE, and indeed the students involved would make up by far the greatest proportion of PCE.

If you are therefore teaching in further education, adult and community learning, workplace learning, or in 14–19 provision, but not employed by a school, you are working in Post Compulsory Education.

Still not that simple, is it? That is the reality of PCE.

What and where you may be teaching

As you can see from the previous section, in a sector as diverse as PCE, teachers will tend to encounter a broader portfolio of teaching experiences across a relatively short period of time than in other sectors of education. To give you something of a feel for how it can be, here are six examples of imaginary but representative teachers to think about.

MEGAN

Megan works as a full-time teacher in a large city-centre further education college and co-ordinates National Vocational Qualification (NVQ) hairdressing courses at Levels 1 and 2. Most of her time (75 per cent) is spent teaching groups of about 20 full-time students, some in mixed-level sessions where students are aiming for either a Level 1 or Level 2 award, and some in sessions specifically for one level alone. Megan also has six hours each week teaching a group of 14-year-old school pupils who are at the college full time, based around an introduction to hairdressing.

The college salon and its associated teaching rooms are her base area and they have recently been refurbished. Megan has desk space in a shared office with three others in the hairdressing team, and sole use of a desktop computer. The rest of Megan's teaching time is split between teaching an evening class which runs one evening a week throughout the academic year, and workplace training, visits and assessments to assess and internally verify NVQ candidates working out in the local area. Megan has 820 teaching hours per year.

DARRYL

Darryl is employed as an employee engagement tutor on a 0.6 part-time contract, funded for two years, by the local authority community education department, and has a base in a small rural community education office. He has responsibility for promoting education and training in literacy, language and numeracy to employees in a largely rural geographical area. Most of his teaching time is spent out in companies and community venues delivering taster courses and basic skills workshops either in the companies' own premises or in one of the network of three learning centres in the area. He also works as an online tutor for a special pilot 'getting to know the Internet' course, which has been developed as part of a national project for engaging 'hard to reach' adult students.

His office is small and shared with two others (who are also often out) and hasn't been decorated for some time, but he has a state-of-the-art laptop computer and everything else needed to provide him with a 'mobile office' (paid for by the project). He regularly works evenings and weekends and sometimes manages to take time off during the week to make up for that. His overall teaching caseload is associated with the targets set by the project, which contract him to organise and run a certain amount of very short taster courses in the workplace, and assist progression of some of those students on to other courses during the year. He averages 16 teaching hours each week.

ASIF

Asif works full time as an information technology tutor for a further education college, which is one of three colleges in a medium-sized city. His time is shared equally between working as part of a team of three staff in an open-access and open-plan computer lab with 60 computer workstations at the college main site, and a community learning centre some eight miles away in a part of the city recognised as being in a disadvantaged area. This centre has 30 computers and offers a government-branded group of online learning programmes, backed up by face-to-face tutorials from various staff, including Asif.

He has a desk in an open-plan office, used by 15 other staff, and has sole use of a computer. All his teaching involves mixed-ability and mixed-age groups, with individuals from varying backgrounds. There is a variety of qualifications on offer, where students can work through different levels of study independently and are given tutorial support as needed. Because of this Asif rarely uses whole-class or even small-group teaching, and his teaching load is 835 hours per year.

DELORES

Delores works full time as a training officer for a large primary health care trust. Seventy-five per cent of her teaching is based in the trust's training centre at one of its main sites, and she covers the personal skills and customer care components of NVQ training for various front-line trust staff, including health care assistants, security and office staff. In addition she supervises nursing trainees and teaches on a management diploma for new trust staff at supervisor level or above, which is linked to a local university. Most of her group teaching sessions are with 15–20 participants. The other 25 per cent of teaching time is spent visiting staff to carry out workplace assessment and provide workplace-based tutorial support, and this can involve travelling to any of the trust's seven sites.

Delores has her own desk in a shared office space with four other trainers and shared use of two computers between the four staff. Delores has a teaching load of 200 training days per year.

GRAHAM

Graham works as a self-employed trainer providing training and development for employers and employees to assist them with compliance and developing best practice in the area of health and safety. This ranges from short, intensive certification courses to enable employers and employees to meet their statutory requirements for health and safety, to certification for drivers of vehicles such as fork lift trucks, and NVQ assessment and internal verification as contracted by small employers, other businesses and the regional centre of a construction industry national training body. Graham can be teaching in a training room on the small business centre in which he has rented an office, or out in a company's training space, or out on site examining drivers for the practical part of their certification. His sessions can be one to one, with a small group or with a group of up to 24, depending on the training programme involved.

Graham has a new computer he has bought himself and has sole use of this in his rented office, which he shares with another trainer in the same field, who is his business partner. On average, Graham teaches 780 hours a year, but he does whatever pattern of work his clients need him to do. He can have one week or two with no teaching, followed by six continuous weeks of intensive training courses running from Monday to Saturday each week.

SUNITA

Sunita is employed on a 0.75 full-time contract in a small further education college, where she teaches psychology. As it is a small college, she teaches on a variety of courses, ranging at the lowest level from GCSE Psychology to a psychology component in the college's new Foundation Degree programme, set up in conjunction with a consortium of colleges and universities in her area. She also contributes psychology to the Access to Higher Education course and an Advanced Vocational Certificate in Education. As a result she teaches a wide range of age and ability levels, but generally in discrete groups ranging from 14 to 25 in size.

The college main campus is undergoing refurbishment and a new building is being added at present, which has put pressure on room space, resulting in Sunita teaching in 14 different rooms across her weekly timetable. Her office space has also been affected, so Sunita is combining working from a home office with 'hot desking' (i.e. using shared desk space) with eight other staff in her department. Sunita teaches 600 hours a year.

These six examples give you a real idea of just how varied and diverse the sector is. There are many other roles, responsibilities, timetables, locations and job descriptions for teachers in Post Compulsory Education, including those working with basic skills, students with disabilities or learning difficulties, police and armed forces trainers and many more. As you can see, however, a teacher's life in the sector is generally varied and you are unlikely to be bored!

THINKING POINT

What's yours like?
Using the same format as the pen pictures we have just considered, think about your own teaching situation.

● How is it similar and how is it different?

● Why do you think there is so much variety?

● Does this make you feel like part of a sector with a wide range of richness?

The student body of Post Compulsory Education

Describing clearly the student body in PCE is a difficult task, as there is no real set of statistics which covers the whole sector, as we have already shown. There are some key trends in learning activity which can be identified, and they include the fact that over 80 per cent of students overall are adults, 60 per cent are female, and over two-thirds study part time. There is also a growth in young people staying in education or training. Participation in learning tends to decline as age increases. The groups most likely to participate in learning are young people, those in paid work and those who stayed in full-time education longer and left it with better qualifications. The groups least likely to participate include those aged 50 or over, those looking after family or home, and those leaving school without qualifications (DfES 2003a and b).

Just from this snapshot you can get some sort of appreciation of the nature of the student body of PCE and that you may genuinely teach a 14-year-old and a 94-year-old in one week. Although many students are adults, more full-time students are young people, so you may well be teaching them more often than adults. Some groups in society are less represented than others, which is covered in more detail in Chapter 11. Overall, PCE has a good record of working with the disadvantaged and in raising achievement, widening participation and adopting inclusive approaches to learning and students. Diversity, as with teaching, is also the key with the students in PCE, as we will often encounter as we move through the book.

References

Armitage, A., Bryant, R., Dunnill, R., Hayes, D., Hudson, A., Kent, J., Lawes, S. and Renwick, M. (2003) *Teaching and Training in Post Compulsory Education*. Buckingham: Open University Press

DfES (2003a) *Education and Training Statistics for the United Kingdom*. London: Department for Education and Skills

DfES (2003b) *National Adult Learning Survey 2002*. London: Department for Education and Skills

Fawbert, F. (2003) *Teaching in Post Compulsory Education – Learning, Skills and Standards*. London: Continuum

Handy, C. (1995) *The Age of Unreason*. 3rd edition. London: Arrow

IDATE (2003) *News 244*. France: IDATE Foundation

Mobile Operators Association (2003) *History of Cellular Mobile Communications*. London: MOA

Teaching and learning starting points

This chapter introduces some key ideas relating to teaching and learning to help you understand the learning process and how you will manage that process as a teacher to support and develop learning. A clear explanation of one of the most common theories about how people learn is then provided using the model of the wheel of learning. We continue with examples of how your teaching can help students get on the wheel of learning to develop new skills, understanding and personal autonomy. Teaching students now takes place in many locations which are not accurately described by the term 'classroom' and the chapter concludes by using the term 'learning site' as a more accurate description of the places in which we teach today.

What is learning all about?

We've got this far into the book and have already mentioned teaching and learning many times. Now is the time to pause and provide some basic starting points in terms of principles and practices, which can give you a framework to make sense of some of the theories of learning, while being able to relate it directly to your practice as a teacher.

> ### THINKING POINT
>
> **Good news and bad news**
> Pick out an experience of learning during your life which you remember as being positive and another which you remember as being negative. Think carefully and go back as far in your life as you wish.
>
> - What was it about those experiences which made them positive or negative?
>
> - Was it something about how you were taught, who taught you, who you were learning with or how you were treated as a person?
>
> - What did you learn from the experiences, how did you learn it and why do you think the learning took place?

Learning experiences

The point of the exercise above is that learning experiences are extremely powerful influences on people's lives. Someone who did very badly in an exam when they were 11 years old can be scared of exams for the rest of their lives. The day your teacher told you that the story you wrote about your family was one of the best they had ever read still makes you feel happy years later. Always remember,

if past learning experiences are very powerful for you, they will also be for the people you are teaching. Take that into account right from the start.

The 'official version' of teaching and learning

Before we introduce our own guide to one of the theories about how people learn, let us start with the 'official version', or at least a series of questions about teaching and learning which you should be aware of right from the start of your teaching career. Like schools, publicly funded provision and providers in PCE are inspected by the government. The Common Inspection Framework (CIF) is the set of questions which inspectors use when assessing provision in all education. The Office for Standards in Education (OfSTED) and the Adult Learning Inspectorate (ALI) carry out inspections across the sector. The questions are undergoing revision during the time this book is being published and are moving towards becoming even more wide ranging in what they include, so I have reproduced the key points here in some detail. The five key questions about teaching and learning are:

1   How well do students achieve?
This includes:

- success in achieving qualifications, learning goals and workplace skills;
- the development of skills which contribute to their social and economic well-being;
- their behaviour and attendance;
- their spiritual, moral, social and cultural development;
- whether they make a positive contribution to the community.

2   How effective are teaching, training and learning?
This includes:

- effective use of teaching, training and resources;
- the suitability and rigour of assessment;
- the diagnosis of, and provision for, additional learning needs.

3 How well do programmes and activities meet the needs and interests of students?

This includes:

- the extent to which programmes or activities match students' aspirations and potential, building on prior attainment and experience;
- how far the curriculum meets external and internal circumstances;
- the contribution of enrichment activities and/or extended services.

4 How well are students guided and supported?

This includes:

- the care, advice, guidance and other support provided;
- the quality and accessibility of information, advice and guidance to students;
- the contribution to the students' capacity to stay safe and be healthy.

5 How effective are leadership and management in raising achievement and supporting all students?

This includes:

- the effectiveness of performance monitoring, quality assurance and self-assessment in achieving improvement;
- the effectiveness of leaders and managers in contributing to improvement and promoting high-quality care, education and training;
- promoting equality of opportunity and tackling discrimination so that all students achieve their potential;
- the adequacy and suitability of staff, specialist equipment, learning resources and accommodation;
- ensuring value for money;
- linking effectively with other providers, services, employers and other organisations.

(ALI/OfSTED 2004: 3)

Just when you thought you were here to teach maths, car maintenance or history, along comes the Common Inspection Framework and makes your task about as big as it can get! The vision of teaching and learning as it features in the framework is almost all-encompassing, with not only the expected inclusion of achieving qualifications but also of benefiting the community, developing moral and spiritual growth, and even maintaining a healthy lifestyle. You may not disagree with these being there, but you would have expected perhaps at least some of this to be someone else's responsibility. Some of it of course will be. Just put yourself in the position of those providing large sums of funding for PCE, such as the government or a student, parent or employer. Wouldn't you feel the CIF questions were ones which you were entitled to ask?

Indeed, as a teacher working in the system, wouldn't you want to ask them yourself? The student is undoubtedly placed at the centre of the teaching and learning process in this model, and as a teacher your role can be seen to be the key contribution to meeting the needs of those students, as stated in the general question of the CIF.

STRATEGY FOR SURVIVAL

Ask those questions!

As the book progresses, more help with matters related to inspection is featured, but at this stage there are three key points to hold in your head:

- Get to know the systems, processes and procedures your organisation has put in place to prepare for inspection.

- Ask the CIF questions about what you do and make sure not only that you can answer them but also that you have access to evidence to support the answers.

- If you keep yourself organised and keep your admin up to date you will probably find inspection a lot less stressful.

The wheel of learning

Charles Handy, who has a useful knack of making the complex accessible, recounts an experience of being taught which goes something like this. You go into a room with a number of other people and sit down. The teacher spends most of the lesson talking to or at the class of students, who are expected to sit and listen, make notes and ask questions only if they don't mind standing out from the crowd or are very confident. Later on in the year, you are asked questions about the content in an examination or test. If you manage to repeat what the teacher was saying, it should mean you have learnt it.

We will all have had experiences like this and indeed we may well have even learnt from them. Handy suggests however that learning is about more than that and I agree wholeheartedly with that idea. David Kolb (1984) described learning as something which builds and grows as we accumulate experiences in our life, reflect on them and adapt our behaviour as we learn new things. He explained this through the use of a 'learning cycle', which has four stages and I have adapted this into my own 'wheel of learning' (see Figure 3.1). The four stages are **experience**, **reflection**, **theorising** and **experimenting**. Although Kolb argues you need all the four stages to take place, they need not always happen in the same order. They can happen very quickly or can take a great deal of time, and they do at times interweave and overlap.

1   Experience – this first stage on the wheel is having an experience, which may be new or may be one you have had before.

2   Reflection – the second stage is where you reflect on the experience and whether it worked well or not.

3   Theorising – the third stage of the wheel is theorising, where you compare your reflections on the experience with your existing store of experiences, ideas and understandings, or your own personal theory, and you start to separate out what might be new and what adds to your previous learning. You may also recognise where the learning is not new and may not proceed beyond this point.

4   Experimenting – the fourth stage of the wheel is experimenting. Having started to build your own personal theory from the reflections and theorising, this is where you try out the learning in different situations, in a deliberate way, to see if and where it works. If it works well it is added to your collection of skills and understanding, if not you may need to go back a stage or two in the cycle to try again.

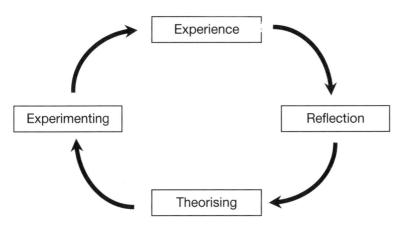

Figure 3.1 Wheel of learning

To some degree this oversimplifies learning, but as a teacher, using the wheel as a way of helping you organise and manage learning with your students can work really well. There are many ways which the wheel of learning could be disrupted for individuals, including personal circumstances. Think of your role as trying to keep your students (and yourself) on the wheel of learning. As Handy (1995: 48–9) says, this type of theory of learning can:

> emphasise how difficult true learning is and why the sort of deliberate change that goes with learning is so rare. This sort of learning, the one from experience and life, is the one which matters if we are to change.

The wheel of learning in practice

We can now use two representative examples of students in PCE to explore the wheel of learning.

A brush-up-your-English student

A woman of 35 has plucked up the courage to come to your evening class because she has got a promotion at work and is struggling with the level of English needed, which was not part of her old job.

At an initial meeting, she explains she needs to be able to write letters to customers on a computer. She has a computer at home but is not very confident with using it and her children are on it most of the time. This student has chosen to get on the wheel of learning herself by identifying joining your class as an experience which could help to solve her problem at work. You suggest she takes a look at a workbook which contains exercises on writing the right type of letters and works through them with your help on one of the centre's computers. A web site with worked examples and interactive exercises about planning and writing letters is also available. She can sign up later for a free online course in 'writing skills for work' if necessary.

You provide a menu of various learning experiences, but how far the student goes with them is essentially her choice. She chooses to work through some of the exercises and tries out the web site, with you providing support. This **experience** takes two or three sessions, with her regularly talking to you about how it is going, and this shows her moving on to the second stage of the wheel, that of **reflection**. At the end of the third session you agree to chat for a tutorial and this provides an excellent opportunity for the student to talk through her reflections so far. She feels she has grown in confidence but needs to check whether she has improved enough to cope with what is needed at work. This shows she has moved on to the **theorising** stage of the wheel and is starting to build her personal theory as the new experiences and reflections combine. She feels she has now learnt what is needed but needs to move on to the final stage of the wheel, which is **experimenting** with the learning in practical situations.

After the tutorial she decides the best way forward will be to enrol on the 'writing skills for work' online course. Over the next few weeks she continues to come to the evening class, where you work with her on various tasks and exercises to improve her writing skills, and she completes and passes the writing skills class. Visibly growing in confidence she chooses to join the next level of computer class and to register for a Level 2 literacy qualification.

This student has made her own use of the wheel of learning and a number of real changes have taken place, which have gone beyond the possibilities raised from the initial problem with learning. She has not only successfully moved through all stages but has continued by progressing on to the first stage again and further experiences which will develop further learning. Your assistance has been crucial in helping the student manage her experience.

A 14-year-old school excludee

You are teaching a vocational skills course, including basic training in information technology, engineering and key skills, with a group of school pupils who have been previously excluded from school. One student is particularly disruptive and challenging from the start and does not settle down at all to work, so you take him to one side at the first opportunity for a one-to-one session. You have decided to use the wheel of learning at the **reflection** stage because this student already has such a powerful accumulated history of non-learning. You firstly reinforce that he is breaking the ground rules which all participants agreed to before attending, then try to clarify whether he understands the limited choices which are available to him, which are either to attend these classes or be excluded from school. In doing this you are trying to encourage reflection on the situation and the consequences of continuing to be disruptive. On being asked whether he expects college to be the same as school he indicates he isn't sure what to expect, but that 'it couldn't be worse'. The pause for reflection has helped him to use the **theorising** stage of the wheel, where, despite the fact that his personal theory suggests this will not work, he recognises that trying out the college course is the choice to make. You negotiate that the **experimenting** stage will involve continuing with the training sessions and agreeing to meet a second-year student who had settling-in problems the year before. In this case the **experience** stage is used last to test out the learning from the other stages.

Over the next two days the student works reasonably well, attends the meeting with the second-year student and selects what appear to be appropriate option choices. You encourage further use of reflection, theorising and experimenting by working directly with the student and using positive feedback and support. The challenge of maintaining self-discipline proves too much, however, and he is suspended from the course for three days after verbally abusing another student and one of the other teachers. In this case the student effectively 'fell off' the wheel of learning during his experience because his personal theory and the resulting behaviour were so strongly established.

The management of the wheel of learning was sound and it gave the student a real opportunity to take responsibility for his own learning. With a repetition of the same approach, using smaller steps at a time, even this student could make progress.

Journeys on the wheel of learning

Think again about the positive and negative learning experiences from earlier in the chapter and consider them as journeys on the wheel of learning. Where did you start on the wheel and what made the process through the stages successful or unsuccessful? What would have to change in order to turn the negative experience into a successful one?

Stay on the wheel of learning

Given what we have said about learning not always working out or being positive, and the wheel of learning not always turning smoothly, the same is bound to be the case for you as a teacher and as a student. It is important to retain a sense of balance here.

You are providing opportunities for students to join the wheel of learning but they may not always wish or choose to take them. That is their choice and not your fault.

As a teacher however you will be presented with many opportunities to learn as an individual and a professional so:

Don't forget to stay on the wheel of learning.

The future of the classroom

The term 'classroom' stills conjures up a particular image. Rows of desks are arranged in lines, there is some form of board at the front and a desk which the teacher can sit at. The students stay in their places the whole time, apart from when it is time to leave at the end of a session, and the teacher shares their wisdom from the front. There are still many teaching rooms in PCE which would look like that if you walked into the empty room as a visitor. They will vary in condition from the sparkling new to the old and grey, and some will have state-of-the-art technology installed, but the majority probably won't. Much excellent teaching and learning does go on in what we are describing as 'classrooms' all around the world, and this section is not intended to suggest otherwise. As a teacher in PCE, however, expecting to teach only in 'classrooms' would never prepare you for the variety of situations and locations in which you may work.

One of the biggest research projects about further education, the Transforming Learning Cultures in Further Education (TLCFE) project, used the term 'sites of learning' or 'learning sites' (Bloomer and James 2001), which in many ways describes more accurately the locations where you may teach in such a diverse sector. A learning site for our purposes is 'a location in which teaching and learning takes place'. This may or may not be a classroom. Some teachers spend part of their day (or evening or weekend) teaching anywhere in the world, without moving from their computer, through the medium of technology. This phenomenon is known as 'classrooms without walls' (McLuhan 1964).

It is the case that many teachers will still spend most or all of their time teaching in the same room, in the same building, for all of the time they teach, and there is no suggestion that this is a bad thing. For many teachers today the classroom as described at the start of this section is a thing of the past, and in future describing a generic classroom is likely to become even more difficult.

THINKING POINT

Your learning sites

To help you move away from the idea that all teaching takes place in a classroom, think of or write down the 'learning sites' or different locations in which you normally teach over a period of two weeks.

- How many of them actually are what you would call 'classrooms'?

- What are the advantages and disadvantages of working in the different types of learning site?

- What kind of an atmosphere for learning can you help to create?

List as many of the other learning sites in which teaching takes place across your organisation as you can.

- How many of them do you think you would be able to adapt to working in?

Some of the answers you may have come up with include:

- a practical teaching area such as a motor vehicle workshop, hair salon, kitchen, laboratory, studio, shop, art room, performance space;

- a lecture theatre;

- a gymnasium or sports hall;

- outdoor sites such as gardens, grounds, sports venues;

- workplaces such as hospitals, factories, small businesses, offices, shops;

- specialised IT facilities such as community learning centres, computer suites, open access areas, learning resource centres.

STRATEGY FOR SURVIVAL

Making the most of learning sites

When you look at this list, you can see that many classrooms are already without walls in the conventional sense, but they are all what we have called learning sites. Whatever range of learning sites your teaching takes you to, you need to make the most of them for the benefit of your students. Here are some tips which can help:

- Check out the spaces you will be teaching in before you use them.

- Find out the facilities, resources and equipment which are available to you and make sure you can use them.

- Check existing risk assessments of the space or carry out your own.

Just remember,

it is just as possible for high-quality learning to take place in a poor learning site as it is for poor-quality learning to take place in a high-quality learning site.

References

Adult Learning Inspectorate/Office for Standards in Education (2004) *Revised Common Inspection Framework for Inspecting Education and Training.* Coventry/London: ALI/OfSTED

Bloomer, M. and James, D. (2001) *Educational Research in Educational Practice.* Paper presented at the Regional Conference of the South West of England Learning and Skills Research Network 3 July 2001. Dartington Hall: Totnes

Handy, C. (1995) *The Age of Unreason.* 3rd edition. London: Arrow

Kolb, D.A. (1984) *Experiential Learning: Experience as the Source of Learning and Development.* Englewood Cliffs, New Jersey: Prentice-Hall

McLuhan, M. (1964) *Understanding Media, The Extensions of Man.* New York: McGraw-Hill.

PART 2

Don't panic

Meeting the initial challenges

This substantial chapter offers practical guidance on how to take a 'don't panic' approach to the early stages of a new teaching post, and provides a 'survival kit' under the title of 'Get inducted'. This includes key strategies for settling in and finding out the things you need to know (and probably a few you'd rather not!) about your role, your job and your organisation. Understanding and developing student motivation follows as the next topic, including what every teacher should know about motivation. The area which is always crucial for new teachers – planning – is introduced, with some simple planning approaches, and the chapter closes by introducing the idea of the teacher as an actively critical professional. By the end of the chapter you will be at least a little less submerged in the deep end.

Get inducted

When you arrive at any new job, especially if it is your first, it naturally takes a while to settle in and get to know how things work. Meeting and getting on with your colleagues and managers is all part of your education about where you fit into the scheme of things. What would be ideal would be a less-pressured period of time at the very start to meet the right people, reflect, prepare your teaching and generally get organised. Something like a pleasant journey on your own wheel of learning. Such a structured settling-in and induction phase would indeed be a great help.

You will get a well-structured and supportive induction from the best employers, which will really help you meet those initial challenges.

Often though you will start your work in PCE 'in at the deep end'.

Post Compulsory Education is a sector which moves at a very fast pace, where the curriculum can change from term to term, let alone year to year. With a diverse and often challenging student group, and at times a bewildering array of bureaucracy to burden your desk (if you have one), starting new teaching can often feel very pressured. The quantity of teaching each member of staff has on their timetable also tends to be high right from the very start of any new job and you would be unlikely at present to get much if any remission as a new or inexperienced teacher. For many people starting their teaching in PCE, induction is more likely to be you starting work on one day and teaching to your full timetable with little official support or guidance on that same day. Phrases like 'up the creek' and 'without a paddle' spring to mind and can often be heard when new teachers join teacher training courses. There are some signs this may be changing, but until a proper induction becomes a legal requirement, change will be slow.

If you add together the key pressures mentioned in this section your first period as a teacher may feel more like being trapped on a large roller-coaster rather than being on the 'wheel of learning'. A significant number of people do, however, like riding roller-coasters, and there can certainly be some similarities in the raw energy created as you loop the loop, and the positive energy from a good early teaching session in a new job is not dissimilar from the adrenalin rush of a white-knuckle ride. There are steps you can take to make the ride as a teacher smoother and less of a shock and to make that settling-in phase more effective and less hectic.

First, in the immortal words written on the front of Douglas Adams' famous *Hitch-Hiker's Guide to the Galaxy* (1979),

'Don't Panic'.

Second, adopt what we shall call the 'get inducted' approach.

Induction and standards

Since September 2003, newly qualified teachers (NQTs) in schools have to be assessed against a set of induction standards (TTA 2003). NQTs need to meet the requirements in order to complete their induction period satisfactorily. The standards relate to areas such as working professionally and sharing practice, using professional development to improve your effectiveness as a teacher, effective planning, managing student behaviour and recognising and working with students with particular needs. Unfortunately such a structure does not yet exist in PCE and of course with many 'trainees' already employed when they start their training but not yet qualified as teachers, it couldn't in the same way. There is much to be said however for a consistent national approach to induction for teachers in PCE, and induction standards as a requirement for employers to meet would be a real help for a teacher's early career in PCE. In their absence, this book provides a less formal 'get inducted guide', which you can consider to be the 'deep-end induction standards'. I have made use of existing induction standards to inform the content and adapted them for my purposes. Your goal should be to arrive at a point where you can genuinely feel you have got inducted through a combination of training, networking with colleagues and peers, and asking your line manager for information, support and guidance which you are entitled to. If, of course, the official sources of induction don't give you all you need, the advice is:

> seek out and make use of your own 'official' and 'unofficial' sources of help and information, as they will all be needed to help you arrive at the 'don't panic' stage.

THINKING POINT AND STRATEGY FOR SURVIVAL

Settling-in quiz

This is the longest Thinking Point in the book, but at this stage it needs to be. Do not do all of this in one go as we want to reduce your panic, not increase it.

You probably knew a certain amount about the organisation you are working for before you started working there, but the settling-in quiz below will certainly help you to become more informed. It will help you settle in and understand your work and your organisation better. The Strategy for Survival is to make sure that where you come up with unanswered questions, you produce your own action plan to follow up where you need to. You'll need to ask these questions:

- How and where can I find out?

- Who can give me the answer?

- Who will give me the answer? (They may not be one and the same.)

- When will I get the answer?

Part One – the 'official' induction

- What induction have you had and what has been included?

- Who are the key people you have been introduced to/made aware of (senior management, head of department, mentor/s, your course team, other relevant teachers, learning support, technical support, external verifiers)?

Part Two – the 'official' information

Much information about educational establishments is now available in the public domain, on the Internet, in the press, and published in print, either as marketing material or in the form of inspection reports, league tables, etc. You should be able to find this either in your learning resources centre/online or in local public places such as libraries. Try to find out the following about your organisation:

- How has the organisation fared in recent inspections?

- What projects/research/development activity has the organisation been involved in and where has it been documented or published?

- Where is the organisation placed in league tables?

- Do any departments or sections have a reputation for excellence or some form of special status (e.g. Centre of Vocational Excellence, involved in European project/s, Beacon Status)?

- What image is presented by the promotional marketing materials?

Part Three – the 'unofficial' induction and information
Some of the crunch questions are about how your own and your students' experiences compare with the 'official version'. Think about your experience and ask around your other colleagues and your students to answer these questions.

- How has your experience compared with the 'official versions'?

- What appears to you to be the student view of the organisation and the teaching and learning in it?

- What is the reputation of the organisation internally and in the local community?

- What is the morale of staff like?

- Who can you go to for help and advice as unofficial mentors?

- Who should you avoid going to?

- Where can you access up-to-date documents and resources for your courses and curriculum?

- How well do the IT facilities work and how effective is the technical support?

- What are the best training courses to go on and why?

Don't forget the action plan!

Working with your students

As I have mentioned before, the students in PCE are as diverse a group as you can teach anywhere in education and they can be equally diverse in terms of behaviour and motivation. All through your teaching career, you will need to be able to work with students who may range from highly motivated to completely apathetic. They may even be present in the same group at the same time every week and they may even be the same person at different times. To be able to work only with motivated students would be great, but in some ways probably less rewarding, as the challenge of stimulating motivation is a positive one. You will mainly try to manage student motivation to give all students an equal chance to learn, but developing ways of motivating your students is also an effective way of reducing disruptive or challenging behaviour.

A motivated student is unlikely to be disruptive.

We consider challenging behaviour in more detail later in the book. For now we will concentrate, as we have throughout this chapter, on some introductory approaches and principles.

Susan Wallace (2002) argues that young people, who are significantly increasing in number in PCE, while appearing to be there out of choice are actually choosing what is potentially the 'lesser of the evils' they are facing. Everyone who joins a learning programme, whatever their age, experience and background, will at some point encounter barriers and problems which will affect their basic motivation to arrive at your teaching sessions, let alone to take part enthusiastically. Don't you sometimes wake up and think, 'Do I really have to get out of bed today?' The people who are your students will also have days, hours or moments like that. It's just that some have them more often than others. This is really important because:

> Student motivation and appropriate behaviour are prerequisites for teaching and learning and in order to address either of these issues, we have to know something about our students as learners. (Wallace 2002: 3)

Developing student motivation

Wallace (2002) presents a range of useful principles and strategies for working with students to develop their motivation and manage their behaviour, which centre on restoring their 'sense of agency' and giving 'them (back) some degree of choice'. The most important of these at this stage of the book is getting to know your students, which is mainly about communication, not about initial assessments or needs analyses, although those have their place.

If you want to understand why your students act in the way they do, you have to listen to what they have to say, observe how they behave, and talk to and with them.

This can be difficult, especially with some students and when you are faced with inappropriate or challenging behaviour. It is however crucial (and eternally interesting) if you can be a dispassionate and objective observer and listener at the same time as teaching (in as much as anyone can be fully dispassionate and objective). In simple terms, if you can develop an understanding of your students as individuals and as a group, and can combine that with the correct approach, planning, methods and resources, you will be able to reduce barriers to learning and maintain student motivation.

Maslow and motivation

Understanding motivation in some detail is extremely useful in that mission of knowing 'something about students as learners' (Wallace 2002: 3). Abraham Maslow (1987) described motivation as a 'hierarchy of needs', which he argued is a series of ascending stages towards achieving true potential, or 'self-actualisation'. The stages are normally represented as a pyramid, with our most basic human needs such as safety, warmth, sleep, water and air towards the base of the pyramid, and self-actualisation, or the capacity to realise our full human potential, at the top. The process of achieving our true potential at the top of the pyramid can be seriously affected if the needs at the lower levels are neglected. In its simplest form Maslow's Hierarchy, when applied to teaching, suggests that if students are cold, uncomfortable, unwell or miserable, that will be a barrier to them achieving their learning potential. Not an idea we would want to disagree with. Maslow's ideas can be seriously questioned, but as one of a number of useful ways of looking at learning, they can be genuinely helpful.

Figure 4.1 and Table 4.1 illustrate Maslow's Hierarchy of Needs and its general relevance to teaching.

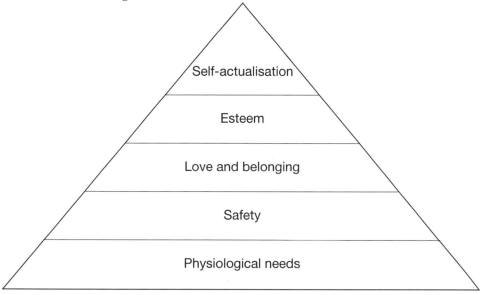

Figure 4.1 Maslow's Hierarchy of Needs

Table 4.1 Maslow's Hierarchy – levels, explanation and relevance for teaching

Level of need	Explanation	Relevance for teaching
Self-actualisation	The desire to reach what you believe to be your full potential	Are the students operating with initiative, autonomy and creativity? Is there an individual and shared sense of achievement?
Esteem	Self-esteem through achievements and being acknowledged by others	Are the students developing growing confidence and autonomy? Is there a culture of peer support and recognition?
Love and belonging	The need to belong and to be valued	Do the students all feel included? Are they treated with respect by others in the group? Are you using inclusive teaching approaches?
Safety	The need for safety and security in their world and in the world in general	Is the physical environment safe? Are the students feeling happy and secure in the environment? Do they have overall confidence in their teacher?
Physiological	Basic needs such as food and sleep	Are the students tired and hungry?

THINKING POINT AND STRATEGY FOR SURVIVAL

What all teachers should know about motivation

It is possible to produce some simple guidance for all teachers to follow, which will help them maximise student motivation. Taking account of Maslow and drawing on Claxton (1984), this guidance is as follows:

- If people feel threatened they are likely to stop learning.

- You need to be able to recognise what worries or threatens your students and develop ways of making them feel safe and secure.

- Even water takes time to digest.

- Motivated students need to stay motivated.

- You can offer opportunities to learn, but you can't make everyone accept them.

- Your way of teaching always influences what students learn.

- Controlling your students may make your life easier, but helping them control themselves should be your ultimate goal.

- What works really well one day may not work at all the next day.

- What works really badly one day may work really well the next day.

Be ASSUREd with your planning

Wherever and whatever you are teaching, you always have to plan. Being able to effectively plan learning activities, sessions and programmes is one of those things we all have to do on a regular basis. Different aspects of this book address various aspects of planning, but this part of your 'get inducted' toolkit provides two simple models to help with your planning.

The first is the 'ASSURE' model, which makes use of Gagne's (1985) ideas relating to the 'conditions of learning'. He argues learning is influenced by both the internal conditions of the student (e.g. their experiences, attitudes, capabilities) and the external conditions (e.g. the way the teaching is organised, the materials used, the location). Until relatively recent times the teacher has tended to be seen as the expert who imparts their special skills and understanding to fill the 'empty vessel' of the student. However, the notion of a teacher as someone who helps students to learn for themselves is now prevalent in most teacher education across the world. The ASSURE model of planning is a series of steps you can work through to focus on managing those internal and external conditions in ways that will most effectively develop learning which is more student-centred. The stages of the model are outlined below.

Analyse students

This first step is all about being aware of the needs and characteristics of your students. Much information is collected about your students as they enrol and you will learn much about them as you teach them. You will also need to devise or use activities to collect information to help with analysis of your students. Some of the information, and how you may collect it, includes:

- age, ethnic group, gender, entry level – this is normally collected when students enrol and should be available to you from your organisation's central administration;

- prior knowledge, skills and attitudes – some of this information may be available if students have been involved in entry assessments or are progressing from other organisations. You can also collect it through group and individual activities, profiling, tutorials and discussion;

- particular circumstances or needs – this again could be collected as students join, but can be essential to understand students and work with them effectively and may need extra activities as above. Legally we are all required to make 'reasonable adaptations' to meet particular needs such as disability, so it is important to be able to access that information;

- learning styles and preferences – many organisations now carry out assessments of these and can help discover, for example, whether students prefer visual approaches or hands-on approaches to learning.

Take learning styles into account in your planning but don't overemphasise their importance.

State objectives

Once you know more about your students, you can write the learning objectives for the session/course. Objectives state what the students will be able to do at the end of the session.

Select teaching methods and learning resources

The teaching methods and learning resources are the teacher's tools of the trade which will help your students achieve the learning objectives. Selecting the appropriate mix of methods and resources should be guided by:

- the subject or topic involved and the methods best suited to teaching it;
- the methods which will combine to best meet a particular student's or group's needs;
- accessibility, clarity, presentation and appropriateness of the learning resources for your students in combination with the chosen methods.

Utilise methods and resources

This is when the session actually takes place and you use the methods and resources as planned. Try out any new methods or resources before you use them, and if you are going to use technology, don't assume that everything will work.

Be sure to have a plan B.

Require student participation

It is generally felt that people learn best when they are actively involved in their learning, and the wheel of learning reflects this. However you approach your teaching, it is possible to include active participation. Try using questions and answers, discussions, group work, hands-on activities, projects and other ways of getting students actively involved in the learning of the content. Use participation to listen to your students and allow them to become aware of the content. Create an atmosphere which will help them to learn as opposed to trying to 'teach' them.

Evaluate and revise

This last stage is often neglected but it is the most important one. Considering what worked well in a session and what didn't is a real challenge for us all, although I'm sure we all at least think about it. However, this stage is about acting on those thoughts and indeed on the thoughts of your students. Sometimes the session you thought was planned down to the final detail may not work because of one small problem. More questions than you expected and one computer in a room of 20 which didn't work, and you ended up covering only half of what was planned. On another occasion, you haven't actually had time to produce the new resources you had planned, but a really good discussion ensued where the students got so involved that they solved the problem set in the session for themselves without the need for further resources.

We all have bad teaching sessions or days. This does not mean we are bad teachers.

If you don't spend time reflecting on your teaching and looking for ways to improve it next time around, you will miss out on being able to provide better learning.

SMART objectives

Writing learning objectives is a crucial part of teaching and is another of those areas which new teachers can find challenging. Think of the objectives as the words which clearly describe the learning that will result from your teaching. After all, if you can't clearly describe the intended learning, how are you going to know whether your students have achieved it? The second model, SMART objectives, are probably used more in business and human resource development than in teaching, but they are included here because the approach is clear and relevant and because we have found teachers like using it. Writing objectives, as the

ASSURE model makes clear, is only part of the planning picture, but it is a very important part.

SMART stands for:

Specific – the student can tell what they should be able to achieve from reading the objective.

Measurable – the student will be able to recognise when they have achieved the objective.

Achievable – it is genuinely possible to complete the objective in the time and with the resources available.

Relevant – the objective is appropriate for the student and the situation.

Time bounded – the objective has a time limit for completion.

For example:

1   By the end of the next two sessions, each team of students will devise and deliver a PowerPoint presentation on their agreed topic to the whole student group and collect feedback from the group on their performance using a questionnaire.

2   By the end of this session you will follow the appropriate job sheet to remove and replace all spark plugs in the blue Mini parked in motor maintenance bay 4.

3   After working through the online key skills self-assessment, you will discuss your feelings about taking the test with two other students and report back the results to the whole group.

If you use these tools, planning will get easier. In addition you can use them to look at syllabuses and other programme documents and see how they match up to the **ASSURE** or **SMART** approaches.

THINKING POINT

How ASSUREd or SMART are you?

- Produce a plan for about five hours of teaching using the ASSURE approach. Use the content in this section to check back on it and evaluate it when you have planned and carried out the teaching.

- Write at least six SMART objectives of your own, use them in your teaching and review the results to see how effectively they were achieved.

- Review at least one other course document you work with to see whether it is ASSUREd or SMART.

Being 'actively critical'

Much of your work early in your career as a teacher is intensely practical and you learn a lot from day-to-day successes or problems. Staying afloat by concentrating on getting things done rather than spending too much time thinking about them is the natural reaction for many. We strongly argue throughout this book that

having a way of 'making sense of what you do' is essential for your long-term health and development as a teacher, and it will help your work and build your personal confidence.

As Killen (1989: 49) puts it:

> Having a mechanical approach to teaching may provide a teacher with immediate skill, but the skills of introspection, open-mindedness and willingness to accept responsibility for one's actions and decisions will give teachers the power to go on developing.   (Killen 1989: 49)

At this stage of the book, we are describing this approach as being 'actively critical'. It will help you to work better, feel better, survive longer and achieve more over an extended period. It is not suggested that this is a painless and problem-free process. We are presenting the teacher as someone who is constantly riding the learning wheel, gradually becoming less likely to fall off, and trying to work with others to keep the wheel turning. You will encounter problems and challenges all the time. If you wish to solve some of those problems, you need to be ready on occasions to push at some of the limits, test some of the boundaries and take occasional risks. At times you may even need to put forward ideas and suggest actions which may not be what others want to hear. Being 'actively critical' goes beyond the technicalities of teaching, it is part of your strategy for survival. Later in the book we will take this idea further, but for now, the key characteristics we suggest you should try to develop to be 'actively critical' are:

- a determination to 'stop and think' about what you are doing on an ongoing basis;
- taking an active interest in how you and your teaching fit into the wider world;
- seeing yourself as a researcher who can improve what you do and contribute to the broader picture;
- keeping an open mind and being ready to accept challenges;
- questioning and problematising what you do individually, with others and in your organisation;
- engaging positively in collaboration and partnership.

So when the getting started quiz throws up a person who has already taught a new course you're going to be involved in, go and see them, ask the questions, offer suggestions and make plans. When you go out into the local area and ask 20 people what your organisation does and what they think of it, and only five have heard of it at all, go back and let your marketing department know, and ask your own students the same questions to see what messages they are getting.

References

Claxton, G. (1984) *Live and Learn: An introduction to the psychology of growth and change in everyday life.* Maidenhead: Open University Press

Gagne, R. (1985) *The Conditions of Learning.* 4th edition. New York: Holt, Rinehart & Winston

Killen, L. (1989) Reflecting on reflective teaching: a response. *Journal of Teacher Education* 47 (1) 49–52

Maslow, A. (1987) *Motivation and Personality.* New York: Harper and Row

Teacher Training Agency (2003) *Induction Standards.* London: TTA

Wallace, S. (2002) *Managing and Motivating Students in Further Education.* Exeter: Learning Matters

Access for all – working with Skills for Life

This chapter introduces a major area of work for all teachers in PCE, which is Skills for Life. The chapter starts by briefly explaining the Skills for Life strategy and the scale and nature of the positive challenge this represents for PCE. A simple quiz is included to help you recognise the scale of problems associated with poor adult literacy, language and numeracy (LLN) in the UK and how this challenges all teachers to take an active part in changing the situation. Mini case studies follow of how students' lives are disadvantaged because of difficulties associated with essential skills, with examples of how opportunities to learn can improve and transform their situations. The chapter then offers an opportunity for you to profile your own background, achievements and barriers relating to language, literacy and number. Considering how this has affected your life chances and career to date will help you understand why this is so important for teachers and their students, and help you to relate more closely to your students' experiences. The chapter closes with some key tips for all teachers in working with essential skills.

Skills for Life

Skills for Life is the major national government strategy to improve adult literacy, language and numeracy skills, which was launched in March 2001. This followed publication of what is known as the Moser Report (after the name of its chair, Sir Claus Moser) in 1999, which reviewed the state of what was then called adult basic skills and proposed a number of key objectives aimed at improving the situation. The key thrust of Skills for Life, and the reason why it involves all of us in PCE, is that it is an 'all embracing strategy, covering all 16+ students at Pre-entry up to and including Level 2, discrete and embedded provision, classroom, community and voluntary and workplace learning' (DfES 2001). Ironically, given the importance of this statement, it is not the clearest

English you'll ever come across, so by way of clarification the strategy has five key components:

- drawing together all organisations involved in working towards improving the situation and setting targets for those organisations to ensure progress;
- developing an integrated national curriculum for LLN;
- developing and providing training for teaching staff in Skills for Life;
- significantly increasing the proportion of the population aged 16 and above who achieve qualifications in literacy, language and numeracy up to and including GCSE grades A–C;
- linking Skills for Life with plans to reduce social exclusion of disadvantaged groups in the UK.

What does this have to do with us as teachers?

First, this is probably the biggest overarching policy drive which has ever taken place in PCE, and significant government resources (£1.5 billion over the first three years) have been invested in making it happen. It is not going to go away, and even if you are teaching badminton for two hours a week as part of an adult education course, it is relevant for you as a teacher. You also need to notice the emphasis is from age 16 upwards, so almost all teachers in the sector will become directly involved in some way. As one of the key purposes of this book is to reinforce the status of teaching as a special and life-enhancing occupation, we would strongly argue that all teachers should readily join forces to help reduce the hardship and social and economic exclusion which can be caused by difficulties with LLN.

The Skills for Life agenda is not going away – embrace it with enthusiasm.

What does it mean in practical terms for most teachers who do not specialise in teaching LLN? For all teachers it is about developing 'inclusive approaches to addressing the language, literacy and numeracy needs of their students' (FENTO 2004: 2). For example, if you can help any of your students to improve their confidence with speaking, writing or maths in any way, the chances are that will have a wider positive impact on their confidence and achievements in learning overall.

Skills for Life has clear expectations of all teachers and expects us all to be able to:

- help our students identify their needs in relation to LLN;
- develop approaches to supporting those needs within our teaching subject;
- achieve a minimum level of competence in our own LLN skills to underpin our teaching roles.

The scale of the challenge

When you look at some of the statistics, you will readily appreciate the scale of the problem we face in the UK. On 2004 DfES figures:

- it is estimated that adults with poor LLN skills could earn over £50,000 less over their lifetime and are more likely to have health problems;
- poor LLN skills cost the country's economy £10 billion every year;
- 5.2 million adults (16 per cent) in England have literacy skills below Level 1 (GCSE D–G);
- 15 million adults in England have numeracy skills below Level 1 (GCSE D–G).

THINKING POINT

How big is the challenge?
Try to answer these questions (all asked in a DfES 2003 survey), then take a look at the answers, which are at the end of the quiz:

1 What percentage of people with poor language, literacy and numeracy skills are employed?
10% __   15% __   50% __   67% __

2 How many people in England struggle because English is not their first language?
125,000 __   750,000 __   500,000 __   1 million __

3 What percentage of people with degrees did *not* reach Level 2 (GCSE A–C) or above for language, literacy and numeracy?
5% __   10% __   20% __   30% __

4 Men have higher levels of literacy than women.
True __   False __

5 What percentage of people said they had received training (outside school) for language, literacy or numeracy?
12% __   20% __   30% __   40% __

6 How many people in Britain have learning difficulties or disabilities?
1.5 million __   5 million __   8.5 million __   10 million __

No cheating!!

Quiz answers
1 50%   2 500,000   3 30%   4 False   5 12%   6 8.5 million

What can I do about it?

As with many areas of teaching, starting small can be a good way of moving forward. Clearly on your own you cannot solve the LLN problems of the nation but you can:

- link up with the specialist advisors, tutors and guidance staff in your organisation to get advice, assistance and specialist support;

- search the Internet for 'skills for life'. There are many good ideas and resources out there for this area of work;

- look out for difficulties students may appear to have with literacy, language or numeracy and how that affects their participation in your sessions;

- add 'skills for life' as a category on your session plans – you'll be surprised how soon it becomes a regular feature;

- be unafraid to seek help yourself if you need to improve your own skills in this area – you are not alone.

Student case studies

Just how can the life chances of members of the community be improved though Skills for Life? The following case studies are adapted from those featured in *Skills for Life* (DfES 2001), the government's initial report on this area, and projects funded under the Adult and Community Learning Fund. They illustrate well how skills for life can be addressed in different and imaginative ways to make a real difference. Use the examples to develop your own practice.

ERIC

Eric has spent much of his time at home in Jamaica, though now he is living in England in and around musicians and studios. He has often helped to operate the studio equipment and would love to work as a sound engineer, but has real difficulties with his reading, writing and maths. A friend suggests he goes to the local college for advice and he ends up joining an adult English and maths course. By the end of the first month he has shown a great deal of improvement in all areas and is surprised to find that the course is not just helpful but also an enjoyable social and learning experience. His confidence is growing and he has plans to take the first qualifications on the road to becoming a sound engineer.

DAVID

David is in his late fifties and has had a variety of low-paid, unskilled jobs for most of his life since leaving school with no qualifications. He recently decided he wanted to learn how to use computers and has taken the plunge by joining an introductory course at his local drop-in learning centre. The course covers computers and brushing up on maths, using online study with help from teachers in the drop-in centre. Being able to work at his own pace and in his own time on the course suits David well and he manages to pass the end qualification in less than the normal time. He chooses to go back into factory work but is confident that he will be able to take opportunities to get promoted and signs up for the next level course.

BANGLADESHI GARDENING GROUP

A group of Bangladeshi women who regularly attended their local community centre rarely moved outside of a small circle of their immediate friends and family, and few were able to speak English with confidence. They all shared an interest in growing window boxes, so the centre education worker managed to persuade them to attend a nearby city farm as a group, with an interpreter, to take part in horticulture classes. This really helped them develop their enthusiasm and skills in plant growing, but gave some enough confidence to try basic English classes, with half of the group passing an introductory certificate. At least half of them are planning to join computer classes and the course has provided a bridge into a wider and richer outside world.

There are some key success factors contained in each of these case studies which are essential if Skills for Life is to succeed.

Your own literacy, language and numeracy profile

One really good way of bringing home the impact literacy, language and numeracy have on our lives is to look at ourselves not just as teachers but as individuals. Like any self-reflection, this isn't always an entirely enjoyable experience, but much of what makes you a good teacher comes from the way you make use of your life experiences in a positive way, so please treat this next activity in that spirit.

Don't limit your capacity – if you need assistance with LLN, ask for help.

Skills for Life teaching tips

To conclude the chapter here are some teaching tips which should help you not only with Skills for Life but generally in using inclusive teaching approaches.

- Make sure you are always looking to improve your skills and confidence in LLN.

- Constantly look for opportunities to include LLN within your subject teaching, starting in small ways and building up.

- Assess your students' LLN skills, previous learning and learning preferences or styles in whatever way works for you and does not undermine their confidence.

- Look for approaches and methods of support which provide variety.

- Keep what interests and motivates your students at the centre of what you do.

- Challenge students and welcome success by accentuating the positive.

- Provide regular feedback and reinforcement opportunities and use them to check learning.
- Where students have a disability, treat them as individuals, not as conditions.
- Ask disabled students about the effects of their disability as they are the experts, and listen to what they say.

References

DfES (1999) *A Fresh Start – Improving Literacy and Numeracy.* London: Department for Education and Skills

DfES (2001) *Skills for Life – the National Strategy for Improving Adult Literacy and Numeracy Skills.* London: DfES

DfES (2003) *The Skills for Life Survey – A national needs and impact survey of literacy, numeracy and ICT skills.* London: DfES

DfES (2004) *Skills for Life – annual review 2003–4. Progress in raising standards, provision and student achievements.* London: DfES

FENTO (2004) *Addressing language, literacy and numeracy needs in education and training: Defining the minimum core of teachers' knowledge, understanding and personal skill – A guide for initial teacher education programmes.* London: Further Education National Training Organisation

The 14–19 curriculum

Since the start of the twenty-first century, and largely as a result of the Labour government's education and social inclusion agendas, the 14–19 curriculum has moved to centre stage in PCE. The numbers of 14–19-year-olds (and in particular 14–16-year-olds) being taught in PCE has grown rapidly, and with that growth have come particular challenges for teachers. In 1998/9, there were 80,000 16- and 17-year-olds studying, mainly (but not only) in FE colleges. Figures since then, particularly of 14–16-year-olds who are school pupils but are attending learning programmes in PCE organisations, show significant growth.

It has been suggested that this situation has 'left many staff feeling ill-prepared to cope with the different characteristics of these students' (le Gallais 2004: 140). This chapter is aimed at making sure you are better prepared. To set the context, the chapter first summarises the background and development of the 14–19 curriculum and what we may expect from it in the future. The next section presents a teaching 14–19 checklist, which contains key hints and tips about general strategies and specific techniques to use with 14–19. The chapter closes with mini case studies, intended to provide examples of successful teaching with 14–19 students.

In transition – changes and priorities 14–19

A reasonable question to ask about PCE at present may well be, 'Why is there so much emphasis on 14–19?' For some considerable time governments, employers and education have been concerned about the underachievement of young adults from some sections of society. Since the 1970s, when youth unemployment was very high, successive governments have tried to improve the situation, with mixed results. Authoritative writers in the field (Lumby and Wilson 2003; Keep and Payne 2002; Hodgson and Spours 2002) summarise the key concerns as follows:

- Low participation and achievement – on 2002 statistics (OECD 2004), 76 per cent of 17-year-olds in the UK are still participating in education. This places the UK at 24th out of 28 OECD countries. More than 5 per cent of young people reach the end of compulsory schooling with no qualifications. In addition, Lumby and Wilson (2003: 534) argue that 'the relative chances of those from the middle class and those from semi-skilled and unskilled backgrounds remains much as they were decades ago'.

- The academic/vocational divide – the 'academic' (as represented by the 'gold standard' of A-Levels) and 'vocational' (as represented by the troubled history of National Vocational Qualifications) components of our education system do not have parity of esteem, from either those in education or those outside it.

What is happening to change this?

The two key challenges above have taxed many governments over 50 years or more, but a major government strategy aimed at addressing them has been progressing since 2002 when the Green Paper, *14–19: Extending Opportunities, Raising Standards*, was published. The Department for Education and Skills (DfES) responded with *14–19: Opportunity and Excellence* in 2003. This established the Working Group on 14–19 Reform, chaired by Mike Tomlinson, which produced its final report in October 2004 (DfES 2004a). The Working Group was asked to consider these three key strategic areas for change in 14–19:

- extending opportunities;
- raising standards;
- making recommendations.

The Working Group report has indeed produced major recommendations for change, which could have a far-reaching impact on PCE and work in schools with 14–19-year-olds. The key recommendations are as follows:

- All 14–19 programmes should contain a 'coherent programme' of 'core and main learning'. The core learning will address mathematics, literacy and communication and information technology, and the main learning will be in the chosen academic and vocational subjects and disciplines.
- The existing qualification system for 14–19-year-olds should be replaced by a wide-ranging diploma, which would recognise achievement across each level of a national framework.
- New vocational programmes will be developed in conjunction with employers and others and should include suitable knowledge, skills and work experience.
- Assessment should be mainly teacher-led, with some external testing, monitoring and review.

- Most of the diplomas will recognise and differentiate achievement through the awarding of grades.

- Entry to and progression through the diploma framework will be based on student needs and capabilities to promote challenge and progression.

(Adapted from DfES 2004a)

THINKING POINT

Being Tomlinson

You can now put yourself in the position of Mike Tomlinson and at least pretend you have the power to influence the future of the 14–19 curriculum. As you are old enough to be a teacher in PCE, it is safe to assume that you will have experienced 14–19 education in some shape or form as a pupil. From your experience and what you know of the experience of others, answer these questions:

- Have you experienced the academic/vocational divide?

- How long did you stay in education from 14–19?

- How did your 14–19 education affect your life prospects?

- What changes would you make to 14–19 education if you were in charge?

What does the future hold?

The Working Party recommendations are wide-ranging and of potentially huge significance to all teachers working with 14–19-year-olds. At the time of writing it is not yet fully clear just how many of the recommendations will be implemented. An implementation timescale of at least ten years has been suggested. What is clear however is that

14–19 work will be central to the future of PCE, so teachers need to be well prepared for it.

In as much as we can future gaze, likely implications for those working with the 14–19 curriculum, whether they work in schools or PCE, are:

- information, advice and guidance will need to be well organised, clear and available to all students;

- the emphasis on flexibility and a personalised curriculum has major implications for those teaching within such a curriculum;

- some specialised training for teachers working with 14–19-year-olds will need to be available for all;

- student support for individual students and groups of students will need to be comprehensive and well resourced;

- parents and pupils may have their expectations raised by plans for a much more responsive approach to education;

- partnerships and alliances between providers, employers and others will play a central role.

14–19: the students

One of the intentions of 14–19 reform is to bring a common experience to all 14–19-year-olds, irrespective of where and what they study and their previous levels of achievement. As a recent evaluation of one of the key 14–19 initiatives has stated:

> In practice, however, pathfinders have tended to emphasise provision for the disaffected and/or disengaged and others for whom the academic route through conventional GCSEs to AS/A2s and beyond was considered less appropriate.

> (DfES 2004b: 56)

In the short term at least this provides extra challenges for teachers in PCE, including managing challenging behaviour, developing and maintaining motivation and raising the aspirations of such students. If you find yourself teaching 14–19 students, what are the key strategies and techniques you should use?

The teaching 14–19 checklist

In many ways, this is the 14–19 strategy for survival:

- Make sure you are familiar with the legal and statutory responsibilities of being involved in teaching 14–16-year-olds.

- Liaise with others such as school staff to ensure the legal and statutory responsibilities are met.

- Establish and operate clear and effective systems for identifying 'at risk' students, monitoring attendance and taking action.

- Keep up to date with relevant background information about individual students or groups of students.

- Emphasise the differences between school and PCE which young students have been shown to enjoy (e.g. more adult and relaxed environment, less formal relationship with teachers, smaller class sizes).

- Recognise and take account of the differences between school and PCE which young students may have difficulty with (e.g. not used to greater freedom, more free time, less supervision).

- Ensure you have common and agreed rules for acceptable behaviour across all programmes.

- Plan learning activity which takes account of different learning styles and preferences and which emphasises activity and variety.

- Promote an ethos which recognises and celebrates achievement.

- Get regular feedback from your students about their learning and act on it.

Remember – younger students are human beings too!

Developing potential: 14–19 in action

These mini case studies are all adapted from those freely available from various sources and provide a representative selection of imaginative and effective work within the 14–19 area.

LAND-BASED COLLEGE

A land-based further education college has a range of practical facilities and training opportunities including a working farm, stables, a lake and a climbing wall. The college felt these would be of interest to 14–16-year-olds in local schools. Over two years a successful programme of NVQs has been developed, which attracts more than 120 pupils from several local schools. The critical success factors have been:

- developing and improving information and guidance about the provision, including 'taster' sessions and interviews with college staff;

- timetabling the activities into one-day attendance per week;

- using teaching staff who were volunteers and providing them with training;

- building participants' confidence and self-esteem through relevant and practical activity, and providing access to the wider facilities and services of the college;

- effective communication between the college and the schools.

IMAGINATIVE WORK-RELATED LEARNING ACTIVITIES

A local authority, an employers' organisation, a further education college and a regional tourist board all wanted to develop learning projects and materials for young students. The area of the country relies heavily on tourism, so an extended assignment called 'a day to remember', linked to the GCSE in Leisure and Tourism, has been created. The key components of the assignment are:

- visits to a range of local attractions, including meetings and interviews with staff working at various levels from management to the shop floor;
- reviewing the attractions using a set of criteria devised by the students and awarding them star ratings;
- developing a promotional campaign using the slogan 'a day to remember' and including a leaflet and web site;
- launching the campaign to other students in their organisations and evaluating the results.

The critical success factors of this example are:

- effective partnership working across a diverse range of organisations, aligned to a common goal;
- making full use of learning technology to enliven activity and enhance presentation of student work;
- providing significant autonomy for students undertaking the activity;
- rooting the work in real vocational situations.

THE LEARNING WAREHOUSE APPROACH

This is based on a successful project of the same name. A group of schools, colleges and universities pooled resources to set up a specialist, community-based learning facility, which could offer a range of learning opportunities in up-to-date premises with a range of technology and support services. The building is also used for business meetings and conferences, and has a café, largely staffed by 14–19 students. The environment is adult and upbeat, and a range of subject-specific computer-based learning materials is constantly available in a staffed technology resource centre. The centre is used by over 1,000 14–19-year-old students each year. Careers advisors have a base in the centre, which is regularly staffed.

Critical success factors of this example are:

- a varied group of organisations and authorities working together to finance, develop and support the centre;
- learning programmes and activities which enable participants to progress and achieve at their own rate;
- a different and unique atmosphere which is different from the normal environment the students are used to;
- advice and guidance is available on site;
- other activities for adults take place at the centre.

References

DfES (2003a) *14–19: Opportunity and Excellence.* London: Department for Education and Skills

DfES (2003b) *Education and Training Statistics for the United Kingdom.* London: DfES

DfES (2004a) *Final Report of the Working Group on 14–19 Reform.* London: DfES

DfES (2004b) *14–19 Pathfinders: An Evaluation of the First Year.* London: DfES

HMSO (2002) *14–19: Extending Opportunities, Raising Standards: Summary Document.* London: Stationery Office

Hodgson, A. and Spours, K. (2002) Curriculum learning and qualifications 14–19, in *14–19 Education. Papers arising from a seminar series held at the Nuffield Foundation,* December 2001–January 2002. London

Keep, E. (1999) UK's VET Policy and the 'Third Way': following a high skills trajectory or running up a dead end street? *Journal of Education and Work* 12 (3) 323–346

Keep, E. and Payne, J. (2002) Policy intervention for a vibrant work-based route – or when policy hits reality's fan (again) in Evans, K., Hodkinson, P. and Unwin, L. (eds) *Working to Learn,* pp. 187–211. London: Kogan Page

le Gallais, T. (2004) The 14–19 sector: responding to change, in Coles, A. (ed.) *Teaching in Post-Compulsory Education. Policy, Practice and Values.* London: David Fulton Publishers

Lumby, J. and Wilson, M. (2003) Developing 14–19 education: meeting needs and improving choice. *Journal of Education Policy,* September–October 18 (5) 533–550

Organisation for Economic Co-operation and Development (2004) *Education at a Glance: OECD Indicators.* Paris: OECD

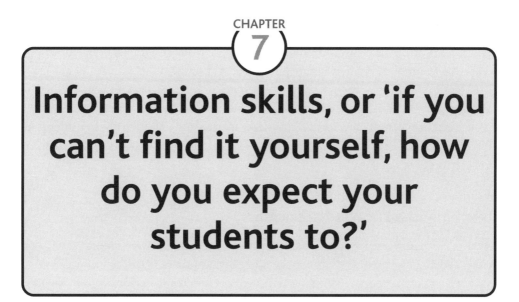

Information skills, or 'if you can't find it yourself, how do you expect your students to?'

This chapter asks some key questions about the knowledge society in which we live and how that impacts on our students and us as teachers. It goes on to suggest that a key feature of PCE should be the development of 'information skills', which can help us empower our students and ourselves by using and actively managing information rather than letting it overwhelm us. The chapter closes with a checklist and Thinking Point designed to help us all develop and improve our information skills.

Information rich but content poor

We are in an age where information is everywhere. On paper it comes through our letterboxes, into our pigeon holes, off magazine racks and news stands, and we can read it while we are at work, at home or on trains, boats and planes. Electronically it comes out of our radios, TVs, DVDs, computers, mobile phones and digital cameras and arrives into our mailboxes and mobiles, and is stored on our voicemail, hard drives, CD-ROMs and Personal Digital Assistants. At times it can feel like information is filling up the whole world, that there are traffic jams on the information superhighway, and that most mail is junk mail. Wherever you are you just can't escape it. (Just like work really.) In many ways, though, the 'information revolution' is a great thing and at its best it can draw people and communities together. At its worst, however, it can represent something of a nightmare, creating a 'digital divide' between people and producing harassment and pressure. The situation we are increasingly finding ourselves in as a society has been described (Goethe Institute 2004) as being in

a media society where we are information rich, but content poor.

Examples of this can be seen in the amount of poor information we encounter in a single day, from junk mail at home, junk email at home and work, and increasingly junk texts. As teachers, we work with information at every stage of what we do, so we must be able to judge for ourselves what is rich and what is poor information. Even more important however is the need for teachers to help their students to make the same decisions, to avoid the problems of what has been described as 'information overload'.

Teaching in a knowledge society

Why do teachers need to pay any attention to this at all? If we ignore it, won't it just go away? The answer to this is certainly no, and there is a much more positive way of seeing the teacher's role as within the knowledge society. What is called the 'knowledge society' is created by a combination of factors including increased globalisation, rapid developments in telecommunications and information technologies, increasing levels of automation in manufacturing processes and a growth in knowledge-intensive business. There are advantages and disadvantages to this, as

> It stimulates growth and prosperity, but its relentless pursuit of profit and self-interest also strains and fragments the social order. Along with other public institutions, our schools must therefore also foster the compassion, community and cosmopolitan identity that will offset the knowledge economy's most destructive effects. The knowledge economy primarily serves the private good. The knowledge society also encompasses the public good. Our schools have to prepare young people for both of them.
>
> (Hargreaves 2002: 1)

Although this argument is presented for schools, continuing this approach to education through the process of lifelong learning and into PCE is equally important.

Education is seen as a primary force for promoting and developing the positive and connecting forces of the knowledge society, and reducing the negative forces of fragmentation and division.

Such a vision of education does present some major new challenges for teachers, and they will need to be working in areas such as:

- developing values and emotions to build character;
- emphasising emotional as well as cognitive learning;
- building commitments to group life;
- cultivating curiosity about and willingness to learn from other cultures;

- developing responsibility to excluded groups within and beyond one's own society.

(Hargreaves 2002: 4)

There is a direct relationship between this approach and information skills as 'the key to a strong knowledge economy is not only whether people can access information. It is also about how well they can process information' (Hargreaves 2002: 3). If teachers are to help with this, the argument is clear. 'Today's teachers must get a grasp of, and a grip on, the knowledge society in which their (pupils) live and will work. If teachers do not understand the knowledge society, they cannot prepare their (pupils) for it' (Hargreaves 2002: 2).

What are information skills?

Nottingham Trent University (NTU) offers a clear and accessible definition, which is:

> Information skills are transferable skills which enable individuals to:
> - recognise a need for information;
> - select appropriate tools for addressing the information gap;
> - locate, access and evaluate the relevant information.
>
> (Nottingham Trent University 2003)

Information is seen as something which should 'enhance student learning and encourage a critical, analytical and evaluative approach to information sources . . . enhancing autonomy and the ability to learn' (NTU 2003). It is genuinely empowering, and we would surely want to help our students to become empowered. This is not only relevant at the upper ends of the education system. It is important also to remember that the term 'information' relates to information in general and in all its varieties, not just the electronic forms. Many of our students are completely immersed in the information age, whatever their level of education, economic status or motivation. But at times they are so immersed they do not think about the quality of the information involved or whether there is any real point sending a video message to someone else in the same room. Consider these questions about your students:

- How often do they arrive at your sessions already equipped with those enhanced information skills listed at the start of this section?

- When they use the Internet, how often do they say that they have looked for information but not been able to find it?

- How often do students introduce information into their work which they have just accepted at face value, without being at all critical about its usefulness or even its factual correctness?

Without labouring the point we would suggest that, irrespective of how convinced you are by arguments about teaching in the knowledge society, poor information skills waste almost as much time in the education system as anything. Improving them should therefore at the very least save us all time and effort, and who knows, we may empower some students and teachers along the way. We cannot do this however unless we improve our own 'information literacy' as teachers.

What can we do to improve the situation?

First, as a teacher, encourage your organisation to prioritise and provide training and support for developing information skills (often the province of the library, which when given the opportunity will probably do an excellent job of this, as they are 'information professionals'). Second, make sure you are confident in your use of information skills. With effective approaches to locating information, you can actually save much time and will rarely (especially with access to the Internet) come away with nothing. Third, what simple tips can help? If you were to search the Internet for the term 'information skills tutorial' you would find much useful advice and information. The set of questions below is a ready-made tool to help you and your students improve information skills.

Information skills checklist

- Be clear about what you need to find out and why you need to know it.
- Make use of what you know already.
- Ask for help if you need it.
- Keep in mind how much time you have available.
- List the places you are able to search for information.
- List ways of checking that what you get is what you need.
- Once you've collected information, separate out items which really match what you need.
- Get the key points from the information.
- Make sure you can go back to the source easily.
- Check what you understand by talking it through with others.
- Make use of the information as you need to.

THINKING POINT

The tortoise and the hare

This exercise is both powerful and fun and can be done either with your students or your colleagues. It will tell you a great deal about information skills.

- Select two teams. One can only use the Internet (the Hares), and the other (the Tortoises) anything else in your Learning Resources Centre (or the nearest you have to an LRC) apart from the Internet.

- Ask both teams to find out the same information (this can be on almost any theme from football to politics) in 15 minutes. They then need to summarise this back to each other.

- Make sure that the information can be found by both methods before you set the task, and try out the searches yourself first to get a good feel of what they are likely to find.

- When the groups come back together, ask them to compare the information, its value and the means they used to collect it.

You may be surprised to discover that the tortoise quite regularly beats the hare.

References

Goethe Institute (2004) *Fly Utopia – Report on Berlin Media Art Festival.* Berlin: Goethe Institute

Hargreaves, A. (2002) Teaching in the Knowledge Society. Keynote paper to *Vision 2020 – second international online conference.* Technology Colleges Trust. Available at: http://www.cybertext.net.au/tct2002/keynote/hargreaves.htm (accessed 4/1/05)

Nottingham Trent University (2003) *Information Skills Portal.* Available at: http://www.ntu.ac.uk/llr/isp.htm (accessed 4/1/05)

8

Positive strategies for managing change

This chapter provides an opportunity to give more attention to the nature of change in PCE and how it can and does affect our everyday work and lives. It provides a guide to positive change management which should help any teacher in PCE both think about and act on the changes they encounter, move more confidently forward in the way they manage change, and work with others towards improving the future.

Being a change agent

In Part 1 of the book, we took a brief look at change and some simple approaches to managing it, but given how much change is an everyday part of PCE, we can now return to it in more detail. Michael Fullan writes powerfully about change and teachers, arguing that 'teaching at its core is a moral profession. Scratch a good teacher, and you will find a moral purpose' (Fullan 1993: 1). In many ways, this might seem something of an old-fashioned view when inspection, heavy teaching loads and initiative overload feature so prominently in the life of teachers today. We would argue that what he has to say currently has even more importance, as things will surely change for the better only if teachers are in some way actively involved in the change process. Fullan's message is that teachers can be 'change agents' and should be involved in 'making a difference' and 'bringing about improvements', which is in tune in many ways with much of the prevailing rhetoric about quality improvement and social inclusion. He continues to say that 'those skilled in change appreciate its volatile character and they explicitly seek ideas for coping with and influencing change' (Fullan 1993: 1).

PCE, despite constantly being immersed in change, does not have a great record in terms of developing its teachers as change agents or supporting them through times of change. Given the levels of bureaucracy and pressures of work, simply maintaining the status quo is at times enough to keep us all very busy for all of every day. There are nevertheless ways in which we can work with change, and even drive change, so let's start here.

THINKING POINT

The journey to change city

Think of a major change which has taken place in your teaching situation in the recent past, as if it has been a planned journey to a destination, which for the purposes of this activity we have called 'change city'. Visualise the whole journey, from plan to arrival at the destination. Track the journey through the stages suggested below and try to plot this visually to get an overall picture of how the different stages took place. (Be imaginative!) Ask these questions to help:

- Choosing the destination.

  Who came up with the change and the rationale behind it?
  (Did you or others plan the journey? Why was that destination chosen? Was the cheapest means of travel chosen, or first class, and why?)

- Choosing and informing the passengers

  Who was affected by the change?
  How and by whom was the change made known to all involved?
  (Why were you in the group of passengers? When and how did you find out about the journey plans? Was there any scope for changing them at this point?)

- Check-in and departure

  As the change approached, how did arrangements for its implementation take place?
  (Was check-in quiet, calm and organised? Were there delays, overbookings or cancellations? Did you depart on time?)

- The journey

  As the change took place, what went well and what not so well, and what support was available?
  (Did you keep to time? Was there in-flight catering and movies or did you have to entertain yourself?)

- Arrival and claiming your luggage

  Overall did the change take place effectively, and what might you alter next time around?

  (Did you arrive on schedule? Was luggage lost or damaged? Would you book with a different company next time?)

  Looking at change as this kind of journey can be revealing and can also help you plan more effectively for the next change you face.

Guide to positive change management

This approach to change is based on developing personal confidence about your work, sharing and developing that with others, and using it to ensure you work more effectively with your students and your peers. It's a combination of developing individual inner strength and assertiveness to survive independently, and making use of strength in numbers so that you can always find other colleagues to support you and share the load. Remember, we are trying to keep you on the wheel of learning with your students because we feel that will make you a better teacher.

The process of positive change management involves four components.

Building your personal vision

This is all about asking yourself why you came into teaching and what difference, if any, you hoped to make. It may not be all that clear and once you start work as a teacher it may be even less so, as the fog of newness descends and the demands of the job bite.

At least once a week ask yourself these three questions:

- What difference have I made this week?
- How do I want things to be next week?
- What can I do to make that happen?

This may or may not make you feel immediately better or lead directly to you doing a better job, but it

> gives meaning to work, and it exists independently of the organisation we happen to be in. Once it gets going, it is not as private as it sounds . . . the more one takes the risk to express personal purpose, the more kindred spirits one will find.
>
> (Fullan 1993: 3)

Obviously not all the answers to the questions will always be positive ones, but you may be surprised at how often, in some way, you are making a difference. Even when the going is tough, that gives you the resolve to keep going.

Persistent questioning

This is not about being the person who always puts their head above the parapet (and usually gets shot as a result), nor about moaning (much as that can sometimes be quite therapeutic), but much more a reinforcement of what we considered earlier as being 'actively critical'. It involves looking for ways of understanding what's going on and learning from it. Questioning what we are doing, and using those questions to reframe, adapt and move on, can be really helpful. This is especially true when we find ourselves in what Schon (1983) called the 'swampy lowlands' or the messy areas of our work (and the 'swampy lowlands' are everywhere in PCE!). Questioning and thinking about what you do will not always be easy and may lead to choices and possibilities which are painful, but we would argue that being prepared to ask the questions is a choice we should all make. Here are more questions to ask at least once a week:

- What are the most positive and the most negative events which have happened in my work this week?
- Why did they happen?
- How can I repeat the positive and avoid the negative next time around?

This is all adding to your store of experiences which you can make use of in your teaching, and helps you to sort and sift what works and what doesn't.

Mastery

Mastery at a simple level is about being skilled and knowledgeable in your field, but Fullan (1993: 5) argues mastery is 'necessary for effectiveness, but it is also a means for achieving deeper understanding'. He also questions how much emphasis and value is placed on mastery in teaching in saying 'it is surprising how little attention we pay to it beyond one-shot workshops and disconnected training' (p. 6). We shall address more aspects of mastery in Part 6 of the book, but add these three questions to those you can ask yourself each week, only this time answer from the point of view of your students.

- What has got better for my students because of what I have done this week?
- What else would they still want me to improve?
- How can I develop towards mastery in that area?

As a teacher you are also an expert in a specialist subject and in the overall business of developing and supporting learning. Mastery is an important part of that expertise.

Collaboration

Developing your personal mental strength, as well as a generally positive outlook, is important, but positive change management does not ignore the value of working with others. 'Personal strength, as long as it is open-minded . . . goes hand-in-hand with effective collaboration – in fact, without personal strength collaboration is more form than content' (Fullan 1993). Think about when you successfully work with other people. When it works best, isn't it often when everyone can be themselves to some degree, while at the same time respecting the others in the group and working together towards common goals? Here is a final set of questions to ask yourself each week about collaboration:

- Who have I successfully collaborated with this week?
- Who have I had problems collaborating successfully with this week?
- How can we work together to reduce the gap between the two?

Try out this approach to positive change management in various ways and in various situations, and ask the questions with colleagues or in a group. You will probably be pleasantly surprised at the common ground which develops. You may also need to say 'no' a little more often (not a word which teachers anywhere are expected to say frequently), but be ready to explain why.

References

Fullan, M. (1993) Why teachers must become change agents. *Educational Leadership 50*, March, 1–13

Schon, D. (1983) *The Reflective Practitioner: How professionals think in action.* New York: Basic Books

Mentoring matters

Mentoring is more prominent as an issue in PCE, particularly since OfSTED's survey inspection report on Initial Teacher Training in Further Education in 2003 found that 'many trainees, particularly those on part-time and fractional contracts, are left to fend for themselves, without adequate mentoring or wider forms of organisational support' (OfSTED 2003: 14). This chapter presents definitions and key principles of mentoring and explains how and why it can be of great value to teachers, their students and their organisations. We will introduce you to examples of how mentoring should work in practice and provide your own 'get mentored' checklist, to help you make sure that you get the support you deserve. The chapter ends with a brief consideration of the potential for online approaches to mentoring.

What is mentoring?

Mentoring is essentially a very simple idea, which is that

a less experienced person will benefit from time and support given by a more experienced person.

This is hardly a revolutionary idea and happens to us all during our lives in our contacts with friends, family, colleagues and others. How often have you learnt something new from someone else more experienced or helped someone else in the same way? Aren't parenting and being friends at their best something like mentoring? Mentoring of school teachers in the early stages of their careers is well established, but the picture in PCE is much more variable.

There are meaningful definitions which can help establish what we should expect from mentoring, including:

Mentoring is the 'deliberate pairing of a more skilled or experienced person with a lesser skilled or experienced one, with the agreed-upon goal of having the lesser skilled person grow and develop.' (Murray 2001)

Mentoring means guiding and supporting the trainee to ease through difficult transitions; it is about smoothing the way, enabling, reassuring as well as directing, managing and instructing. It should unblock the ways to change by building self-confidence, self-esteem and a readiness to act as well as to engage in on-going constructive interpersonal relationships.

(Fletcher 2000: iii)

'the focus (of mentoring) is to identify the key characteristics of an excellent teacher in further education and second, to suggest how such excellent teachers can encourage others towards excellence.'

(AoC/FENTO 2001).

These definitions reveal some of the tensions, contradictions and complications which can beset mentoring. Is it mainly for the benefit of the new teacher or for the organisation? Is it about personal growth and development or is it about skills and quality assurance? Just how important are the skills of the mentor and how can we develop them? A positive experience of mentoring can make a real difference, just as easily as a negative experience can be disastrous.

No mentoring at all may actually be better than poor mentoring, which can do more harm than good.

THINKING POINT

Mentor or dementor?

If you're not sure where the title for this Thinking Point came from, just ask anyone you know who has children between about six and fourteen. Work on this activity with someone else. If you have not started teaching yet, make sure you pair up with someone who has.

- What do you think are the most important purposes of mentoring?

- How would you expect to be treated as a mentee and how do you think mentoring could best be organised for you?

- What skills and training would your mentor need?

- In what ways would a mentor be able to help you develop your subject-specific teaching?

- How might all of this be recorded as part of your training and professional development?

- How does any of this compare with your actual experiences of mentoring to date?

You will probably find some of these questions difficult to answer, as getting access to a suitable mentor could be extremely difficult if you work in a small organisation or subject team. If you happen to be the only teacher of Japanese in an organisation, is a very experienced teacher in another subject or another less-experienced foreign language teacher the best person to mentor you?

Why mentoring?

At its best, mentoring will certainly be beneficial to both the mentee and the mentor, but it could also significantly impact on your organisation in a number of positive ways. Research on mentoring in PCE is limited, but a joint venture between the Association of Colleges (AoC) and the Further Education National Training Organisation (FENTO) in 2001 produced a useful set of materials, which aimed to help institutions and their staff develop fuller and effective approaches to mentoring. In this publication it suggested that mentoring should:

- link up with other quality improvement strategies;
- connect with other professional support and development opportunities;
- help to develop policies and procedures which are understood more widely and which give staff a more shared ownership of them;
- ensure that the right people become mentors, that their roles are clear, and that they are suitably trained and supported;
- improve communication across the institution and help build a feeling of a 'community of practice'.

This helps to provide our definition of mentoring, which is:

one of the key factors for new staff, which helps them and their organisation operate more smoothly, communicate better and value each other more, in addition to being something of a focus for developing and celebrating excellence.

How mentoring can work

Mentoring has many dimensions and will be different in many ways for each person being mentored. To help give an idea of what can be involved, here are two examples of the ways in which positive mentoring can work in practice. They should suggest some approaches you may be able to try or ask your own mentor to develop.

New teacher of health and social care in a small further education college

You're two weeks into your new job, teaching on a variety of courses in a small department, where there are two others in your immediate course team. You have been allocated a mentor who is an experienced tutor in your field, but who does not directly teach with you on any courses. He does work at the same site as you and his office is in the same building. You were introduced during your induction day and spent about 25 minutes talking about when the regular weekly sessions and observations will take place and agreeing an action plan for the first month. You've already made informal contact with him by email and telephone three times since to ask specific questions, which have either been answered straight away or shortly afterwards.

At your first formal meeting you agree to sit in on one of his sessions as an informal observer, and set a date for him to do the same with one of your sessions this week, before your first formal observation. When observing his session you can see he has a bank of regular sources and resources for his students to use when putting together assignments and presentations. He has collected them on some internal web pages, so the students have easy access, and he has a filing cabinet of other resources in the classroom. Most of the sources are relevant to what you teach.

He has a problem getting over a particular part of the session and when discussing it afterwards, you suggest a way you think it could have been taught to make it work better next time. He agrees to give you access to the resource bank, but adds to your action plan that you should create and locate some more to be added to what will become a shared resource bank. You clarify what will be involved in the session he will sit in on, write up your mentee log about your first two weeks and file it on your Record of Achievement for your teacher training course.

Work-based trainer in a hotel

You work as a supervisor in a large hotel and spend half of each week training staff in the workplace in food hygiene, customer service and housekeeping. Most of them are working towards NVQs and you are also an in-house assessor and internal verifier. You have registered for a Certificate in Education to improve your qualifications and it is a requirement of the qualification that you have workplace mentoring from a subject specialist. There is not a suitable subject mentor available in your workplace, so you have been allocated one from a regional pool, which has been organised by a consortium of local training providers and teacher training centres. Your mentor has 20 years of experience in the trade and she works as a full-time trainer/co-ordinator in the training centre of a major local employer. She is available to you through a schedule of fortnightly visits to your workplace, visits to her office by prior arrangement, telephone contact, email contact and a virtual learning environment specially designed to support this kind of regional-based mentoring. If she is not available you have a mentoring help desk number at the consortium to contact for advice.

At your first meeting you raise the fact that you have regularly encountered problems trying to assess staff who are almost always on different shift patterns from you and your mentor agrees to discuss with your line manager the amendment of shift patterns to make assessment more possible. She will also encourage your employer to use the grants available locally to train more assessors.

You have a half-hour break from training so log in to the virtual learning environment and join a discussion group in your subject. Another trainer at the other end of the region has come across a complication with interpretation of performance criteria in a unit you also assess, and you join the discussion. The mentor moderating the discussion asks if anyone has any advice and you are able to pass on information you got from an external verifier visit a short time ago, which will solve the problem. In return, the other trainer emails a new resource to the group, which is an excellent new web site.

'Get mentored' checklist

If you are working in a small organisation in PCE, getting a mentor allocated to you could be a major problem, as you may be the only person working in that area in your organisation. Even if you are, for example, working in a large further education college, you may still be in a team of five or six, all of whom are teaching most of the time, or possibly not in the same place at the same time very often. The 'get mentored' checklist will help you to make mentoring work for you.

The mentee

- Make sure that you have your own 'informal mentors', who are trusted and helpful colleagues whom you can and do go to for advice.
- If you are allocated a mentor, make sure you have someone else to go to if things don't work out in any way (the 'escape hatch').
- Protect the regular times with your mentor as appointments you never miss.
- Remember to be 'actively critical'.
- Take the initiative to look for mentor support in other places as well (e.g. professional associations, subject-based web sites and electronic forums).

The mentor

A mentoring scheme will not work without time and resources invested in it at all levels. Close links between human resources and professional development should also exist in terms of organisation, training and deployment of mentors. Criteria for mentors should include (adapted from AoC/FENTO 2001):

- a commitment to championing best practice;
- broad experience of teaching and a good understanding of how students learn;

- a sound depth of subject expertise;
- enthusiasm and readiness to share and develop ideas and approaches;
- ability to listen actively and respond effectively;
- effective organisational skills.

> ### STRATEGY FOR SURVIVAL
>
> **Get a mentor!**
> Take an active approach to getting an entitlement to mentoring which corresponds to the checklist. If you are not happy in any way, approach human resources, staff development and your senior line managers to suggest that you need to 'get mentored' and ask what they can do about it. If this is an intimidating approach, ask someone else (such as your line manager or teacher trainer) to do it on your behalf.

Online mentoring

Some of the problems associated with mentoring in PCE centre on local availability of suitable mentors and access to a broad range of expertise in your subject. Both these problems could potentially be eased through the use of online mentoring. By using tools and technologies which are readily available, it would be possible and practical to:

- organise groups of mentors in different subject areas;
- collect, create and index libraries of subject-related resources;
- facilitate individual and group contact between mentors and mentees in different geographical locations;
- develop interaction around subject-based and generic teaching issues which can take place independent of the geographical location of the participants;
- assist the development of subject-based (and cross-subject) 'communities of practice' of teachers.

This is a new and relatively untried area, and ensuring the high quality of personal interaction between mentors and mentees would be its biggest challenge. We feel it does however provide a genuine opportunity to make the most of emerging technologies to assist the development of this key area of PCE.

THINKING POINT

Could online mentoring work for you?

Return to the comments you came up with in our earlier Thinking Point and the 'get mentored' checklist. How much help (or hindrance) do you think online mentoring could be in your teaching situation?

References

Association of Colleges (AoC)/Further Education National Training Organisation (FENTO) (2001) *Mentoring Towards Excellence.* Coventry: Learning and Skills Council

Fletcher, S. (2000) *Mentoring in Schools: A Handbook of Good Practice.* London: Kogan Page

Murray, M. (2001) *Beyond the Myths and Magic of Mentoring: How to Facilitate an Effective Mentoring Process.* San Francisco: Jossey Bass

OfSTED (2003) *The Initial Training of Further Education Teachers: a survey.* London: OfSTED

PART 3

Surviving in the classroom

Developing your specialist subject

This chapter first considers the huge array of qualifications and courses which are available in PCE and how grouping them into subject families could be a helpful way of making more sense of them all as specialist areas. We then continue by asking what being a 'specialist' can mean to you as a teacher, and the values and practical approaches which can help to place your subject at the centre of what you do. I ask you to think about the particular responsibilities that your specialist subject gives you as a teacher, and explain some of the techniques for putting over your subject, or communicating it effectively to your students. The chapter closes with some thoughts about how learning technology could make developing your subject specialism and networking with others more possible in the future.

Just how 'special' is your subject?

If you asked about 30 school teachers at random in one secondary school what their specialist teaching subject was, a list of about 10–12 different subjects would probably be the result. If you asked a similarly random group of 30 teachers in a medium-sized further education college or adult and community learning service, you would probably end up with a list twice as long. Some of the key reasons for this are:

- the diversity and variety of organisations operating in PCE;
- the differences which can exist within the particular types of provision offered;
- the extensive range of subjects which can be on offer within one geographical area.

In one urban area, for example, there may be six or seven further education colleges, each offering academic and vocational provision, general and higher education. There will probably also be specialised training organisations offering work-based training in subjects such as motor vehicle maintenance and/or construction; centres aimed at supporting adult basic literacy, language and numeracy or computing skills; voluntary sector organisations providing training to their own workers and volunteers; and many employers providing or buying in training for their employees. Finding specialist subject titles and descriptions which cover this variety is a major challenge.

THINKING POINT

Is everything a specialism?

This activity will help you to more fully understand the complex issue of subject specialism. Collect prospectuses from three educational providers in your geographical area. Try to include a secondary school, a further education college and the local adult and community education service.

- Work through them all using a highlighter.

- Every time you see what you consider to be a different specialist subject, highlight the entry.

- Once you have gone through each publication, count how many you have ended up with.

- What differences are there between the number and types of subject?

- Can you group the subjects in any way that makes sense or have the publications themselves used a meaningful grouping?

- Where does your specialist subject fit?

If you did this with a typical medium-sized FE college prospectus, you would see over 600 separate courses on offer. Each of these would not be in an entirely different specialist subject, but you could end up with 200 different specialisms from that one prospectus. Even a small adult and community education prospectus could contain at least 40–50 subjects. A number of 'official' groupings of subjects already exist for various purposes. The most common in PCE would tend to be either the titles of departments in an organisation or the 14 'curriculum and occupational areas' which OfSTED uses when inspecting PCE (OfSTED 2004). Examples of these are 'construction', 'humanities' and 'business administration, management and professional', 'health, social care and public services' and 'visual, performing arts and media'.

Groupings of this type are clearly necessary for all kinds of purposes, but just how meaningful they are to you as a teacher is debatable. If someone at a party asks you about your job, would you say you teach (if you don't mind saying you're a teacher, of course!) 'accounting', or 'business administration, management and professional'; 'life drawing' or 'visual, performing arts and media'? Can we find a more helpful way of grouping subjects, which has some real meaning for teachers and which gives us all some feeling of having a 'special place' within the system? If we could identify agreed, national, meaningful subject groupings and clarify where the smaller, more specialised teaching subjects fit into those groupings, it would be a significant step forward for PCE.

The Consortium for Post Compulsory Education and Training at the University of Huddersfield has actually produced a set of 20 'specialist sub groups' which appear to provide an example of this approach working in practice. The sub groups are used to group teacher trainees as part of a summer school based around subject specialisms. These are not necessarily especially meaningful in themselves, but within each sub group there is an associated list of subject titles, which most teachers would readily see as an acceptable categorising of their own subject. I would strongly endorse the use of 15–20 nationally agreed 'subject families', each with a subset of subject specialisms within that family. Each teacher could be given some choice of which to be associated with and this would form the basis of a national specialist group. Wherever a teacher worked, this specialism could follow them, but allowance could be made to update and review the situation as part of a teacher's career and professional development.

What is different about being a subject specialist?

There are some aspects of teaching a particular subject which will be completely different from one subject to another. If you are teaching horticulture, for example, you are going to spend more time outside with your students than if you are teaching basic computing, and the hands-on environment will be different. If you are teaching on a higher education Post Graduate Diploma in Healthcare Management, you will need a more advanced understanding of academic research and writing in your field than if you are teaching NVQ Level 1 in Catering. Across these examples, however, there are also marked similarities. Horticulture and computing can sometimes overlap in areas such as garden design. Healthcare management and catering both involve people skills. Is this part of what makes them special and different or part of what makes them similar? Tricky, isn't it?

Earlier in the book I introduced the notion of mastery as partly involving 'being skilled and knowledgeable in your field', but also relating to effectiveness in teaching. Depth of subject understanding is one of many dimensions of effective teaching, but I place the emphasis primarily on the effective teaching rather than the subject specialism. My definition is:

A subject specialist is someone who is able to effectively develop, extend and teach their recognised area of specialist expertise,

and who seeks to contribute to their own specialised 'community of practice'.

You could be a foremost expert in your field, but if you cannot communicate that to your students you will not be a successful teacher in PCE.

What, then, makes an effective subject specialist? The following criteria are adapted from work produced by the University of Huddersfield (2003) and the Teacher Training Agency (2004). A subject specialist should be able to:

- help students develop learning in the specialist subject;
- design learning programmes in their subject which take account of current subject and curriculum developments;
- identify, adapt and use specialist teaching and learning resources;
- demonstrate an inclusive approach within their subject;
- recognise the importance of literacy, language, numeracy and learning technology within their subject;
- develop a secure and up-to-date subject base through research, professional development and evaluation of teaching activity;
- work with other teachers in their own subject;
- evaluate their own subject expertise and update it as appropriate.

THINKING POINT AND STRATEGY FOR SURVIVAL

Where are you now as a subject specialist?

Using the set of criteria above, self assess where you would consider you stand currently as a subject specialist. Rate yourself between 1 and 5 (1 being low and 5 high). Bear in mind that if you are a new teacher, you wouldn't necessarily expect to start from a particularly high base, and even if you are a very experienced teacher you should still identify areas to improve. Decide on three steps or actions you can take to improve and set yourself a specific timescale by which to achieve them. Return to the list regularly and see how you do on an ongoing basis.

Putting it over

Whatever the subject, it is reasonable to assume that most of your students want, need or have to learn more about it. A number of them may already have some experience and a sense of confidence they can learn the subject, while others may completely lack confidence in their ability to learn. Much of what a teacher does to break down the subject so that everyone can learn it involves the general skills any teacher uses. These include communicating clearly, building student confidence, effective planning, assessing appropriately and gathering student feedback through evaluation. With a specialist subject, however, comes a range of content which has its own particular nature and complexity, and sometimes it is that new complexity which is most difficult for students. One of the most important aspects of 'putting over' your specialist subject is therefore being able to present complex skills, knowledge and understanding in a way which makes it accessible and relevant for your students. A 2003 consultation document on developing subject specialism with school teachers puts it nicely:

> It is a combination of deep subject knowledge and a range of appropriate teaching and learning techniques which make for the most powerful interactions between teachers and pupils.   (DfES 2003: 2)

Whether you are trying to teach your students how to correctly screw in a screw or how to split an atom, one thing which you normally have to do is to think through how that activity, task or understanding breaks down into separate stages, steps or components. Having done that you need to then use your teaching skills to help each student put together those stages, steps or components in a way that they understand and which meets the learning objectives of the subject. These two parts of the process are what I would describe as 'putting it over' or teaching your subject in a way that engages your students and gives them all the best chance of achieving the learning objectives. The stage of breaking down an activity into stages has been called Task Analysis by Gagne (1985) and is a crucial part of welcoming your students to the world of your subject. If you sequence the steps in a confusing way or find it difficult to take your students through them, important opportunities to teach your specialist subject will be lost. An excellent way of illustrating this is to analyse a task which seems so everyday as to be taken for granted, and to try to teach it to someone else.

THINKING POINT

Cup of tea
Try to task analyse making a cup of tea, then construct a simple plan for teaching someone else to do it. (Remember the ASSURE model and SMART objectives from Chapter 4). Imagine they have never made a cup of tea (which of course may be true), then try to teach them how using your plan. Where and why do difficulties occur? It's not as easy as it seems. The activity illustrates well how specialist skills and understanding need to be underpinned by effective communication and teaching strategies.

References

DfES (2003) *Subject Specialism Consultation Document.* London: DfES

Gagne, R. (1985) *The Conditions of Learning.* 4th edition. New York: Holt, Rinehart & Winston

Office for Standards in Education (2004) *Standards and Quality 2002/03. The Annual Report of Her Majesty's Chief Inspector of Schools.* London: OfSTED

Teacher Training Agency (2004) *Qualifying to Teach – Handbook of Guidance.* London: TTA

University of Huddersfield (2003) *Summer School Module Handbook.* Huddersfield: PCET Consortium

Working with a diverse student body

This chapter is about developing approaches and techniques which will help your diverse range of students get the best from their learning both as individuals and as members of a group. Examples are included which illustrate how individual differences can be recognised and accommodated, and individual disadvantages reduced and overcome, with a combination of inclusive learning and widening participation. Scenarios are provided to help you consider how new students can be attracted to your organisation and the role you as a teacher can play in that. The chapter closes with some important advice on ways of setting targets with your students and the helping skills which are an important underpinning of the teacher's role in working with diversity.

Diversity and inclusive learning

In a society such as that in the United Kingdom, great diversity exists. The positive approach to diversity is to see it as a rich vein of varied experiences, values, understandings and skills and which presents society with major opportunities to use the diversity for the benefit of all. Alongside such diversity there is also often inequality, and one of the major goals of PCE is to work positively with the diversity of our students to reduce inequality. If we can recognise, acknowledge and make use of diversity through our teaching, this can make a major contribution to a more equal society.

The two platforms on which I have based my approach to promoting diversity and equality of opportunity are inclusive learning and widening participation. We shall come to widening participation shortly, but let's start with inclusive learning. My definition is:

Inclusive learning is about providing all of your students with opportunities to achieve to the best of their abilities.

In order to be able to accomplish this we need to provide an educational environment which recognises and takes real account of the fact that students have different cultural backgrounds, abilities and disabilities, learning styles, strengths and weaknesses. Alongside this we need to develop educational opportunities that meet their individual and group needs. This is partly about how we as teachers individually organise and carry out our own teaching, and partly about the overall teaching and learning context, culture and environment within which all teachers are working. By thinking about and working with our individual teaching situation and our broader working context, it is possible to create a more flexible and inclusive teaching and learning environment for all.

THINKING POINT AND STRATEGY FOR SURVIVAL

Developing inclusive approaches

Being ready to support inclusive learning involves many different factors, ranging from the configuration and layout of buildings and facilities to the ways in which you communicate with your students and the handouts, books or other materials you use in teaching sessions. This activity will help you to consider some of these factors, rate how inclusive your current teaching situation really is, and plan how you can improve it. Spend five minutes thinking about what any prospective student should be entitled to expect in terms of an inclusive learning experience.

- Don't just think about your situation, think anywhere in PCE. This can work really well if you share your ideas with at least one other person.

- Generate a top ten of inclusive learning approaches from your discussions (don't forget there are now many legal responsibilities which underpin diversity in the UK – include them in your thinking or find out more).

- Applying this list to your teaching situation, give a rating up to 10 out of 10 for each item on the list.

- Looking at the results, identify the main causes for concern and reasons to be cheerful (anything under 5 would be a strong cause for concern).

- Decide what you can do in the next month to improve on one of the causes for concern.

- If it is an area which you cannot directly influence, find out who can and ask them what can be done.

- Draw in others who can help, as there will be help available.

- Come back to the list in a month to see what has changed.

You cannot get away with ignoring this area, as the weight of law is behind it. If you take a positive approach to diversity through inclusive learning, your teaching life and the learning of your students will be much the richer for it.

Widening participation and engaging new students

According to the National Adult Learning Survey (NALS), which is carried out annually by the DfES, '76% of adults aged 16–69 (outside continuous full-time education) had taken part in learning over the last three years, an increase from 74% in 1997' (DfES 2003: 1). Although this is a very positive statistic, the same publication also shows that the same groups who have consistently not engaged in learning over the last 20 years are still not doing so. 'Participation levels are considerably lower than average among certain groups, including: people aged 70 and over (28%), respondents with no qualifications (29%), those with basic skills difficulties (52%) and adults living in the most deprived areas (67%)' (DfES 2003: 1).

What this means is that, despite generally healthy participation rates,

if you are elderly, unqualified, have problems with literacy, language or numeracy, or live in a deprived area, you will be up to 50 per cent less likely to participate in learning than other members of society.

PCE has a very good record generally for drawing in new students and working with more disadvantaged groups, but as these statistics show, there is much still to be done. A greater number of teachers in PCE now work in the front line of the drive to engage new students, as many posts have been created across the sector directly to that end. Even though you may often not work directly in the front line, you may well have students in your groups who are new to learning or are making a fresh start. Taking account of that fact in your teaching is essential.

Widening participation scenarios

These scenarios are based on real projects which engaged groups and individuals who have not been participating in learning. Read the scenario and consider what actions could be taken to engage the students concerned.

Homeless
A group of homeless adults has been selling a well-known publication in town centres, which has provided basic subsistence for the vendors, but has not moved them on from homelessness and out of substance abuse. The voluntary

organisation working with them has approached your organisation for assistance with training to help move their clients forward.

Craft workshop

A local community centre has a group of Asian women who regularly come to the centre and who have expressed an interest in coming together to work on creative textile projects. In many cases English is not their first language and they range in age from 35 to 75. They are not going to want to gain qualifications but would like to give a craft workshop a try.

Employee engagement

You have been appointed as an 'employee engagement' worker and your task is to meet a recruitment target of 100 new students from local small and medium-sized enterprises (SMEs) in your local semi-rural area and to concentrate on training which can enhance the language, literacy and numeracy skills of the participants. What do you do for your first two weeks?

Get engaged

There are published 'characteristics of good practice' in this field (Crawley 2002; LSDA 2002, 2003). We have drawn on these to produce 'get engaged questions' about the teaching aspects of engaging new students:

- Is equality of opportunity genuinely embedded into the ethos and operation of your organisation?
- Are you aware and taking account of your statutory responsibilities?
- What entitlement to practical, financial and learning support is available?
- Are you aware of the profile of your local community and how that is reflected in those participating in learning with your organisation?
- How flexible is the curriculum and teaching and learning you can offer?
- Do you feature diversity in your curriculum and planning?
- Does your curriculum promote progression in clear and manageable steps?

Target setting

Now you have recruited your diverse group of students, how can you work with them to make the most of that diversity? As a teacher in PCE, one thing you can be sure of is that you will come in contact with targets on a regular basis. There will be targets relating to recruiting and keeping your students, getting them qualified and encouraging them to come back and study more. There are already national targets for widening participation, percentages of people entering higher education, improving literacy and expanding learning through electronic means, and achievement of all of these targets would be a happy occasion. As a 2004 report on evaluation in the voluntary and community sector has commented, however, we have to be careful not to get into the situation where it can become a case of 'Hitting the Target – Missing the Point' (Crawley 2004). In other words,

we must make sure targets assist us in our work to support diversity through learning, rather than get in the way.

Providing real and meaningful challenges to stimulate and motivate our students is one of the most effective means of moving from engagement to achievement. This is where target setting can be really useful. Once we have successfully attracted new students to take up our learning opportunities we would all want to make sure they are helped to stay, progress and achieve. A helpful model of target setting in this context is described by Martinez (2001), who suggests that 'without challenge, students will not be able to achieve to the best of their abilities'. However, this is not a simple task:

> For targets to be both challenging and achievable it is important to consider the process of teaching and learning. Targets need to be negotiated and agreed with the tutor but owned by the student. This ownership has cognitive, emotional and motivating elements. Managing the relationship between challenge and achievability for the individual student or trainee demands a high degree of skill and professional expertise on the part of the tutor.
>
> (Martinez 2001: 1)

Here are some hints and tips for getting to grips with targets in general terms:

● Create targets which can be flexible and adaptable in line with changing circumstances. They must not end up as immovable and unhelpful.

● Make time for target setting, monitoring, review and adjustment.

● Welcome other staff's involvement in setting targets, but keep overall control where you are the lead teacher.

● Use relevant specialist tutorial or support staff as appropriate.

Starting points – S.C.A.M.

Despite the unfortunate acronym, Martinez (2001) provides a really helpful model of target setting. It is similar in a number of ways to the writing of SMART objectives introduced earlier in the book. The starting point here is that

targets should be SPECIFIC, CHALLENGING, ACHIEVABLE and MEASURABLE.

Targets may be set with both individuals and groups, but remember that owner-ship by the student is essential.

Specific

Specific targets have to be informed and up to date, so there is a need to collect and record information to back this up. Every attempt to help your students to self assess should be taken. If you don't know where a particular person is starting from, how can you help them set targets relating to where they could be going next? The backup information will include diagnostic assessments, prior experiences and achievements, expectations, tutorial and progress records, and general goals.

Examples of specific targets could be to:

- achieve 100 per cent attendance for the next module;
- observe the behaviour of one of your brothers or sisters for five minutes and make notes;
- write a letter to book a hotel room for two nights.

Challenging

What is challenging for one student will of course be straightforward for another and this is where a combination of the students driving the target setting and the quality of the teachers' interaction with the student becomes central. You need to negotiate a minimum starting point and take account of any particular course-related or student-related circumstances.

Examples of challenging targets could be to:

- improve attendance from 60 per cent to 90 per cent for the next module;
- practise a minimum of two and a maximum of five of the required welding joints in the workshop over the next week;
- work in a group presentation in a co-operative manner, ensuring equality of contribution.

Achievable

Working out what may be achievable for your group of students is something that you the teacher always get a feel for quite quickly. Each of your students also arrives with their own view of just what they can and will achieve, which may change dramatically for the better or for the worse once they get started. Target setting is a way of establishing what could be described as a 'personal pathway' to achievement for each student, so making sure targets are achievable is crucial. Agreeing the minimum expectations but promoting the idea of exceeding that minimum wherever possible underpins this. We would not want to push our students beyond their capabilities, but equally we would not want them to fall below what they would reasonably hope to achieve. Of the targets already provided as examples, can you identify any potential problems around how achievable they are?

Measurable

Unless the targets are measurable, it is going to be difficult to recognise whether they have been achieved or not, so this stage is about a combination of being clear and keeping good records. Two of the above examples could be made more measurable as follows:

- to provide a signed-off job sheet by next week indicating completion of a minimum of two and a maximum of five practice welding joints from the required selection;
- to provide verbal confirmation from other group members that you contributed in a co-operative and non-dominant manner.

If you still need encouragement, take heart from Martinez (2001: 5) when he says 'the best argument for implementing target setting processes is that they work. The evidence for this comes from two main types of research – large-scale international reviews of educational research on effective teaching and small-scale case studies mainly from England'.

Helping skills

This chapter has addressed inclusive teaching, engaging new students and target setting, all of which are areas of your teaching which require a sophisticated and advanced set of skills, many of which are to do with communicating and interacting positively with your students. What connects all these areas is what are known as 'helping skills' and the way a teacher can operate as a 'skilled helper'. The best-known model in this field is called the Three-Stage Model of Helping and is derived from Gerard Egan's work, including the text *The Skilled Helper* (1994). Egan drew his theory from works by Carl Rogers during the 1970s and 1980s such as *Freedom to Learn*. Rogers was one of a number of people who developed what has become known as the 'person-centred approach', a philosophy in which each human being is unique in his or her own right and sees their own world in their own way. The qualities of empathetic understanding, acceptance and sincerity are seen as essential when human beings relate to each other and can provide opportunities for personal growth.

Egan developed this philosophy into an approach where a skilled helper can assist personal growth through what has become known as the Three-Stage Model of Helping. These stages are:

1 Exploration (i.e. where am I now?).

2 New understanding (i.e. where would I like to be?).

3 Action (i.e. how can I get there?).

The helping skills which are needed to assist others in moving through these stages are complex, but there are some basic helping skills which all teachers would benefit from developing:

- Attending – show visibly that you are attending to your students as a group and individually. This is through a combination of an open and positive posture, making eye contact and being relaxed with them.

- Active listening – pay attention to the content and the feelings being conveyed by your students and acknowledge both.

- Reflecting – mirror what your students are feeling in ways which will help them to understand the potential consequences.

- Encouraging – use ways of getting your students to think for themselves and understand their feelings and actions.

- Questioning – be able to ask questions which clarify and help students focus on making their own choices and decisions, and recognise the consequences.

THINKING POINT

Are you listening?

Think of a situation where you are with a group of other people or an individual. How much do you use the helping skills listed above? Are you an active listener? Do you attend to others? The chances are you won't say 'yes' to all of these all the time, as it demands a huge amount of concentration and the skills concerned are subtle and difficult to acquire.

STRATEGY FOR SURVIVAL

One-minute listening

Practise those helping skills, as improving them can enhance your capacity to interact positively with your students considerably. As usual, start small. Spend one minute listening to another person, then summarise back to them what they have said and how you read the way they felt while saying it. You will be really surprised how much this can improve your capacity to listen actively.

Helping skills are at the centre of inclusive teaching so don't neglect them.

References

Crawley, J. (2002) *Staff Checklist for Widening Participation.* Bristol: University of the West of England

Crawley, J. (2004) *Hitting the Target, Missing the Point.* London: Trust and Foundation News

Department for Education and Skills (2003) *National Adult Learning Survey (NALS) 2002.* London: DfES

Egan, G. (1994) *The Skilled Helper.* California: Brooks/Cole Pubs

LSDA (2002) *Equality and Diversity in Adult and Community Learning – a guide for managers.* London: Learning and Skills Development Agency

LSDA (2003) *Widening Adult Participation: ways to extend good practice. A research report for the Learning and Skills Council.* London: Learning and Skills Development Agency

Martinez, P. (2001) *Great Expectations: setting targets for students.* London: LSDA

Rogers, C. and Freiberg, H. J. (1993) *Freedom to Learn.* 3rd edition. New York: Merrill

Managing challenging behaviour

All teachers will encounter challenging behaviour during their career, and some of it will surely be from their students!

Challenging behaviour can take many forms, from a minor disagreement or excessive verbal enthusiasm in a group, to physical intimidation and even violence in a teaching session. A book such as this cannot provide you with a full set of strategies and techniques to manage that challenging behaviour, but it can give you some worthwhile starting points. This chapter first introduces our broad definition of challenging behaviour, then a well-known approach to group dynamics, which helps understand how groups work, and through that how you can manage your own groups to reduce the chances of challenging behaviour. The chapter then moves on to consider the more extreme types and forms of behaviours which can occur. Key techniques to use when managing challenging behaviour, linked to case studies involving behaviour problems, bring the chapter to conclusion.

Defining challenging behaviour

First, what exactly do we mean by 'challenging behaviour'? It is likely that your own definition will largely depend on when and how you experience it (or even when you behave in a challenging way yourself). Aggression or violence towards you or others; not carrying out tasks or activities in teaching sessions; talking constantly; winding everyone up; disrupting the work of others; dominating a group discussion . . . these could all be described as challenging behaviours. My definition, which is intended to be useful to all readers of this book, is:

Behaviour by individuals and groups which causes others problems, and which limits the potential of all concerned to learn and live their lives in as full and free a manner as possible.

Groups and group dynamics

When people come together in groups for any purpose, it is generally accepted that the behaviour of the group moves through certain stages and changes, some of which are positive and helpful and some less so. If as a teacher you are aware of these changes and can influence how and when they take place, you can help the group function effectively rather than becoming dysfunctional. A widely recognised description of these stages has been produced by Tuckman (1965), which I will summarise here with the help of an excellent explanatory paper from the Catalyst Consulting Group (1999). The four stages are called forming, storming, norming and performing. Any group may move back and forward between stages but is more likely to operate effectively in the last two than the first two. Table 12.1 explains what each stage involves and the implications for the teacher.

Table 12.1 Stages in the formation of a group

Stage and group behaviours	Teacher activity at each stage
Forming	
Their purpose and goals are unclear	Provide opportunities for clarification, information and advice and encourage co-operation to establish common goals
Members feel varying degrees of commitment	Find out more about the group and encourage them to share personal expectations and interests
Members are cautious, don't start things off and avoid responsibility	Clarify rules and expectations including accountability, recognition and rewards
Communication is low and a few members often dominate	Find out who has what to contribute and consider how they may be able to do so
Members are dependent on directive leadership	
Storming	
Differences and confusion arising over goals and roles, and struggles over approaches, direction and control	Involve everyone in discussion and decision making
Reacting towards leadership with counterproductive behaviours	Check out differences, include all ideas and opinions and raise difficult issues where necessary
Uncertainty about how to deal with issues openly	Help to clarify purpose and develop a common approach

Table 12.1 (continued)

Stage and group behaviours	Teacher activity at each stage
Communication is not working effectively and decision making takes place through dominance, power plays and compromise	Help the group make the best use of the personal resources they have
Members act independently without reference to the group	
Norming	
Group gains confidence, feels a sense of momentum	Provide encouragement, build consensus and provide feedback through facilitating open discussion
'What', 'How', 'Who' and 'When' become clarified	Provide opportunities for others to move into leading roles
Agreement by most on approaches, goals, communication and leadership roles emerges	Encourage group to interact more with outsiders
Decision making by consensus with some delegation to smaller sub groups	
Performing	
Members take full responsibility for tasks and relationships and work proactively for the benefit of the group	Help the group to assess and evaluate results of activity against purpose and external requirements
Group achieves effective and satisfying results and recognises that achievement	Celebrate successes – reward and recognise individuals and group achievements
Group becomes self-organising and more independent individually but still able to operate as a group	Promote further improvement within the group

THINKING POINT

Storming or performing?

Consider either one group you teach or one you have been a member of. Using Tuckman's model, track the progress (or otherwise) of that group and how it moved through the different stages. How did you as an individual influence the way the group operated? What could you and the group have done differently?

Just for fun, think about your own organisation as a group of people – where is it currently in Tuckman's stages and why?

Balancing the group dynamic

As the person most engaged in trying to balance the group dynamic towards positive results, there are some simple guidelines you can follow:

- Be particularly attentive to the group in the early stages.

- Promote give and take and some degree of autonomy but step in where forming and storming appear to be negatively affecting individuals within the group.

- Promote peer responsibility. A self-regulating learning group can be much more effective than a teacher-regulated one.

- Expect some ups and downs, as there almost always will be.

- No group is ever exactly the same as another, so be ready for that.

Types of challenging behaviour

Minor aspects of challenging behaviour can be managed in ways which are covered in other parts of this book, so we concentrate in this section on the more extreme examples. Teachers in PCE are being faced with more cases of challenging behaviour as they work more with a diverse and challenging student group, and in particular when they work with 14–19 programmes. In a recent study of school teachers' perceptions of pupils' challenging behaviour, the strength of feeling on this issue was emphasised:

> Results indicate that teachers are concerned about challenging behaviour and find it stressful. Whilst considering themselves to be effective in dealing with it, a proportion report feeling frustrated by it, angry, upset and/or at a loss.   (Male 2003: 162)

Although the study was about working with children with severe learning difficulties, we would want to emphasise that extreme behaviour is not limited to that student group. There are three types of challenging behaviour (adapted from Male 2003 and Biersdorff 2002):

- Aggressive – violence directed at others, or at property. This can include:
  - threatening others physically;
  - fighting or hitting;
  - damaging equipment or fittings;
  - verbal abuse.

- Socially disruptive – actions which make it difficult for individuals to get along well with others or to fit into the community (Biersdorff 2002: 1). This can include:
  - not carrying out actions or tasks;
  - inappropriate language or behaviour;
  - winding up others in the group;
  - dominating and manipulating.
- Personally destructive – physically or mentally damaging actions to their own person. This can include:
  - self-harm;
  - rocking backwards and forwards.

THINKING POINT

What behaviour challenges you?

- What range of challenging behaviours do you face as a teacher on a day-to-day basis?

- How do they affect you, the individuals concerned and your other students?

- How do you manage them?

Working with challenging behaviour

STRATEGY FOR SURVIVAL

Free to learn

This strategy returns to our definition at the start of the chapter and is based on the commitment to ensuring the freedom of all students to learn is not prejudiced through challenging behaviour. There will be varying degrees of severity associated with challenging behaviour, but there are some key strategies which can be used in all cases:

- Establish rules for appropriate behaviour, so that learning may take place (Wallace 2002: 39)

The purpose of the rules is not to ensure compliance but to ensure everyone is safe and the best conditions for motivated learning are in place. Inflexible and punitive rules may well be counter-productive, although some breaking of the rules (particularly externally set rules) will at times involve sanctions or punishment. Your goal should be rules which are not excessive in number, which support learning and can be shared and agreed by your students.

- Go to peace not war . . . our goals are to motivate students towards achievement and celebrate that achievement, not to win a war with them.

On many occasions through this book we have and will come across the philosophy that teachers are seeking to help their students to learn and achieve. This does not disappear because our students behave in ways we would prefer they didn't. Of course some behaviour is genuinely a risk to you and other students, and we accept that appropriate action has to be taken for the safety and benefit of all. An environment which is conducive to learning for all is the goal for us all.

- Stay together . . . make sure that your teaching team and other colleagues (up to and including senior management) take a consistent and common approach.

One thing which can make problems with behaviour more difficult to manage is when different people act differently in response to that behaviour. Training, risk assessment and communication are all essential components in making sure this doesn't happen. With some students, if they can find a weakness in your collective way of working with them, they will certainly exploit it.

- Analyse what's going on . . . gather information about why the behaviour is taking place and plan what can be done to avoid, stop or change it.

Where possible try to anticipate problems and prevent them happening, but also have in place clear procedures and strategies for dealing with them when they do happen. This may often involve information, advice and support from others such as learning support, health and safety and learning resources.

Specific actions

There are also actions you can take and questions you can ask which will make a difference, including the following:

- Assess the potential risks and plan accordingly – risk assessments will result in clear courses of action.

- Why is it happening? – what is the person's history, what triggers can produce the behaviour, how can the environment affect them?

- What is it for? – is this new or established behaviour? Is it to gain attention?

- What effect is it having? – damage to property, personal injury, effect on others.

- Applying the rules – remind all parties of the agreed rules and apply them fairly and firmly.

- Stop it – where risk is greatest, call assistance to intervene or withdraw to minimise risk to yourself and others.

- Diffuse it – use diversionary activity to shift the behaviour into another mode.

- Use available help – working with others is often more successful than working alone. Try to deploy peer/group pressure.

- Review and make changes – review the actions you take and make changes to prevent or stop challenging behaviour on an ongoing basis.

Challenging behaviour examples

This activity prompts you to plan how you could respond to occurrences of challenging behaviour in practice. Read each of the following brief examples. After the third is a list of strategies for managing potential or actual challenging behaviour. Try to match the strategies with the case studies. There are not necessarily exact matches in every case.

KEVIN

Kevin has been excluded from school on numerous occasions due to anti-social behaviour. His social skills and basic skills are poor and he has already returned early from two spells of work experience in companies. He does enjoy hands-on work and has helped his dad at home with some building projects. He can be volatile and disruptive, individually and in a group.

WANDA

Wanda is generally something of a non-conformist, both in dress and behaviour, who is studying AS levels, including Psychology and English. When handing in her personal UCAS statement, she writes it in the form of a novel about her life, including some high-quality creative writing alongside swearing and explicit sexual language.

FIGHTING IN A WORKSHOP WITH TOOLS (FROM WALLACE 2002)

Two students start fighting in a practical workshop where you are teaching, using tools from that workshop.

Possible strategies

- Provide a training programme, including practical training, which can lead to a qualification using continuous assessment.
- Create an opportunity to discuss the behaviour openly and consider the possible consequences.
- Get all other students to a safe place.
- Where intervention can be made safely, seek to calm things down.
- Discuss what to do with your course team and the relevant head of department.
- Ensure a high tutor:student ratio to maintain comprehensive support.
- Ensure appropriate reports/statements are produced as evidence.
- Organise integrated and student-centred support in life skills and basic skills.
- Call police and security.
- Agree a number of possible courses of action, emphasising the final choice (and the consequences) are the student's responsibility.

References

Biersdorff, K. (2002) Meeting the challenges of challenging behaviour. *Rehabilitation Review* 13 (2) February

Catalyst Consulting (1999) *Accelerating Team Development – The Tuckman Model.* Capitola, CA: Catalyst Consulting Group

Male, D. (2003) Challenging behaviour: the perceptions of teachers of children and young people with severe learning disabilities. *Journal of Research in Special Educational Needs* 3 (32003) 162–171

Tuckman, B. W. (1965) Developmental sequence in small groups. *Psychological Bulletin* 63 (6) 384–399

Wallace, S. (2002) *Managing and Motivating Students in Further Education.* Exeter: Learning Matters

13

Putting the 'learning' into e-learning

As we discussed earlier in this book, we are living and working in a technologically advanced and information-rich world. This chapter is intended to help you make the most of the opportunities which e-learning can offer you and your students, whilst highlighting the pitfalls which you will almost certainly encounter along the way. We begin with an explanation of what e-learning is in clear and simple language. You are then asked to complete the 'e-learning . . . enthusiast or sceptic' quiz about your attitude and approach to e-learning. The chapter then presents a strong argument for introducing simple but creative uses of e-learning into your teaching, emphasising the benefits for your students. By following the advice in this chapter you should be able to enrich your students' learning and your teaching and make sure that it is 'learning' which is at the heart of e-learning.

What is e-learning?

The field of technology in education is a rapidly changing one and definitions come and go almost as rapidly as new processors, screens and software. Terms which are used include 'educational technology', 'information and learning technology', 'online learning' and, most recently, 'e-learning'. These all have their own uses (and abuses) and the variety of terminology doesn't help in a field which can also be over-hyped and misunderstood.

I can provide you with two definitions which I feel work best. They are intended to be simple and comprehensive, to take account of current writing and research, but mainly to be useful and relevant for you as teachers. The first of these is learning technology (LT). I simply use the Association for Learning Technology's (2004: 1) definition:

> the systematic application of a body of knowledge to the design, implementation and evaluation of teaching and learning. The body of knowledge, the fruit of research and practice, is based on principles of learning theory, instructional design and change management, but is grounded in an understanding of the underlying technologies

and their capabilities. Learning technology makes use of a broad range of communication, information, and related technologies to support learning and teaching.

This substantial and authoritative definition includes much more than using computers and digital technologies. If you use a video recorder, TV, digital camera, photocopier, telephone, audio tape, CD-Rom or overhead projector you are using LT.

My second definition, e-learning, has recently come to the fore as a generic term. One well-respected definition put forward as part of the Waller-Wilson Matrix is:

> E-Learning is the effective learning process created by combining digitally delivered content with (learning) support and services.   (Waller and Wilson 2001: 1)

The DfES (2003) offers what on the face of it appears to be a simple definition:

> If someone is learning in a way that uses information and communication technologies (ICTs), they are using e-learning. They could be a pre-school child playing an interactive game; they could be a group of pupils collaborating on a history project with pupils in another country via the Internet; they could be geography students watching an animated diagram of a volcanic eruption their lecturer has just downloaded; they could be a nurse taking her driving theory test online with a reading aid to help her dyslexia – it all counts as e-learning.   (DfES 2003: 4)

For the purposes of this chapter, our definition is something of a blend of both:

E-learning is the use of learning technology to support and extend learning.

An essential element of this definition is the way it emphasises learning as being at the heart of the process. One common mistake made in this area of our work is to be seduced by the notion of what tends to be called 'putting the "e" into e-learning'. This is a valuable principle, but we have to be very careful to ensure that in putting the 'e' in, we don't take the learning out.

THINKING POINT

Enthusiast or sceptic quiz

Reflect on our deliberately broad definitions of e-learning and learning technology and think about your home, your workplace and where you spend the small amount of spare time which is left outside your working hours. Don't forget, a fax, mobile phone, electronic till, cash machine, stereo, DVD and calculator, as well as items mentioned earlier, all use LT.

1   In a typical week, what technology do you use which could support learning?

2   How confident are you personally in using these technologies?

3   On a scale of 1–10, with 1 being a sceptic and 10 an enthusiast, where would you place yourself generally in relation to e-learning?

4 Which of these answers is closest to your views?
   a) I have used e-learning successfully and am convinced it is beneficial for student learning.
   b) I get a buzz from using e-learning and try to use it wherever I can in my teaching.
   c) I have used e-learning and will use it more, but need help and support.
   d) When I try to use e-learning, things have a tendency to go wrong, which doesn't encourage me to use it more.
   e) I'm not confident in my use of technology generally and will avoid e-learning if I can.
   f) e-learning is a waste of time and I can get better results without it.

5 How much more do you expect to be using e-learning in your future teaching?

6 Does that prospect:
   a) Fill you with enthusiasm?
   b) Leave you unmoved?
   c) Fill you with dread?

This is by no means a scientific quiz and you should easily be able to work out how much of an e-learning sceptic or enthusiast you are from your score. What it may also highlight are differences between your attitude to teaching in general and e-learning in particular. Are you, for example, confident with using the gadgets and equipment you have at home and work, but reluctant to go along the e-learning route in your teaching, even though it may involve the same technology? Are you something of a technophobe generally but would be delighted if someone would help you start off by teaching you how to use email?

Technology is the tool

E-learning is one of those areas of a teacher's work which tends to generate extreme views and much hype, but is it really worth bothering with? Haywood and Hutchins (2004) argue the positive case extremely well:

> Like any resource, ICT [Information and Communication Technology] can be used creatively, to enhance learning. However, a learning activity does not have value simply because it is approached through a sophisticated technology. An activity which is educationally unsound and inappropriate for the student does not become a good learning experience simply because it is computer based. ICT can be used for impoverished as well as rich learning opportunities . . . It may be tempting to think 'why bother!' The

reason for bothering is that ICT is a medium for developing a range of higher order skills including collaborative learning, collective thinking and building communities of students, whether local or global. It has the capacity to offer challenging and motivating opportunities, when students have access to powerful learning tools. Commercial games manufacturers have taken full advantage of this potential.   (p. 8)

I would offer a slogan here which I hope makes my view as clear as possible:

E-learning is the tool, but learning is the goal.

What works most often?

Is there, then, real evidence to show what works and how you can try it out in your own teaching? Much has been written about the strengths and weaknesses of e-learning, with general agreement that it is 'not embedded in our teaching and learning' (DfES 2003). When we review recent research which is representative of the field, a list of what is argued to work with e-learning emerges (BECTA 2004; Crawley and Attewell 2001; Passey, Rogers, Machell and McHugh 2004).

E-learning does work when . . .

- A step-by-step approach is taken to development and implementation.
- It is used to link people together for collaboration.
- Students use it to help research, writing and editing, and presentation of work.
- It is used as a clear and rapid means of communication between and among teachers and students, particularly through email.
- It makes full use of the available richness of content and interactivity to promote deeper learning.
- It focuses on learning activity, not enhancing presentation of teaching.
- It offers students and teachers opportunities to work at times and in places of their choosing.
- It is linked with literacy, language and numeracy support for students to improve their skills and life prospects.
- 'Assistive technology' is made available for students with a disability or learning difficulty.
- Other approaches to engaging people in learning have not worked.

Many of these reflect what we have already argued about learning, not the technology, being centre stage, so you may wish to try any of the above.

E-learning golden rules

However enthusiastic or sceptical you may be, there are some key golden rules you should always follow with e-learning:

- Make sure you and your students have the IT skills needed to carry out any task or activity.
- Make sure using e-learning is appropriate and relevant.
- All the other aspects of your teaching need to be just as carefully and thoroughly prepared as usual.
- Make sure you have the equipment where and when you need it, and technical support available.
- Always have a plan B – at some stage, if it can go wrong, it will!

Examples of positive uses of e-learning

Having defined e-learning and provided ideas about ways in which it can enhance learning, this section now offers a series of worked examples of how you can try it out in practice.

Photo gallery

Bring in a digital camera to use with a group of new students (making sure you have already checked they don't mind). Ask them to do these things:

- Organise taking a photo of each student which they are happy with, then print them out so that each photo is half an A4 page.
- Ask each person to write a mini biography (50–100 words) without an identifying name and get them all word processed and printed out, again on half A4-sized paper.
- Ask the group to try to match the biographies to the photos, until you have all of them correct.

This can help build group identity, generate fun, develop writing, summarising and discussion skills, and familiarise your students with the use of digital cameras. It can be extended to form a pictorial progress review of the group over a period of time and could develop towards making web pages, mini books and presentations.

Find a forum

This task uses the Internet and already existing online forums or discussion groups.

- Discuss with your group what their interests are and locate online discussion groups or forums which cover those interests, e.g. football, pop music, films, soaps, local history.

- Ask small groups of students to select one (or more) forum which they want to contribute to.

- After checking the 'correct usage' rules of that forum, small groups write contributions which will start a new thread of discussion and enter them on to the forum.

- Each group then monitors the responses over a period of time, and time is set aside for a verbal summary to a whole-group discussion about the results.

This activity can develop students' skills in responsible Internet use, verbal discussion, writing to criteria, and extending of expertise and understanding in the field of their interest. It can be extended into specially designed groups which are solely for your student group and which can become part of your assessment of their knowledge and understanding.

How does it work?

You need to take a group of motor vehicle students through the process of how a car engine works. You have a workshop with a real engine and cars, some of which work, but it has always been difficult to really get this topic over. There are various resources which can show you this in other ways. One of the best is the 'how stuff works' web site, which includes animations, cut-away diagrams and detailed explanations at no charge. You will easily be able to locate this site and others which are similar through a simple search on the Internet.

- Find a source which will help to put your topic over to your students effectively and carefully plan how to use it.

- Get organised to project the web pages live to your students via a projector.

- Make sure that you check out any difficult-to-understand or less effective parts in advance, then run your presentation, using the parts which have most visual impact (e.g. diagrams and animations).

- Build other learning activity around the source to help the students when they are visiting the site themselves as backup for your presentation.

This can provide a high-quality resource at no cost and can bring things to the students which they cannot otherwise experience in one place. Giving students responsibility for finding other sources and sharing them with their peers can be a strong motivator and can build a pool of resources for the benefit of all.

Virtual tourism

Ever visited one of those holiday villa websites which gives you a virtual tour of the properties you would like to stay in? It's now possible to let your students be 'virtual tourists' in many ways through the power of technology. You can visit places and situations which are impossible or impractical to experience in any other way, and bring them alive for your students. Virtual tours you can easily find include:

● Shakespeare's Globe Theatre in London;

● the NASA Space Shuttle;

● No 10 Downing Street;

● experiencing a front-line trench during World War One.

Of course, you have to be careful that there is a point to using such resources, but the growing power and speed of current computers can bring many animations, simulations and other resources to the desktops of you and your students.

We hope these examples of moving on to the 'virtual' wheel of learning have whetted your appetite enough for you to get into putting the learning into e-learning, but just make sure that when you do, you remember to think about how it actually worked and what benefits there were. Always ask:

● What benefits did your students get from using e-learning?

● Did you notice improvements in student involvement, motivation and results in comparison with the use of other learning tools?

● What would you do differently next time?

● Overall was it worth it for you and your students?

References

Association for Learning Technology (2004) *Definition of Learning Technology.* Oxford: ALT (http://www.alt.ac.uk/learning_technology.html (accessed 4/1/05))

British Educational Communications and Technology Agency (2004) *What the Research Says About ICT and Continuing Professional Development (CPD) for Teachers.* Coventry: BECTA

Crawley, J. and Attewell, J. (2001) *Promoting Social Inclusion and Widening Participation Via Distributed and Electronic Learning: A review of the research evidence.* London: Learning and Skills Development Agency

Department for Education and Skills (2003) *Towards a Unified e-Learning Strategy.* Consultation document. London: DfES

Haywood, S. and Hutchins, M. (2004) ICT and learning for the future, in Ward, S. (ed.) *Education Studies: A Student's Guide.* London: Routledge

Passey, D., Rogers, C., Machell, J. and McHugh, G. (2004) *The Motivational Effect of ICT on Pupils.* London: DfES

Waller, V. and Wilson, J. (2001) e-learning statement and matrix, in *Open Learning Today* 58, October 2001. Letchworth: British Association of Open Learning

PART 4

Surviving outside the classroom

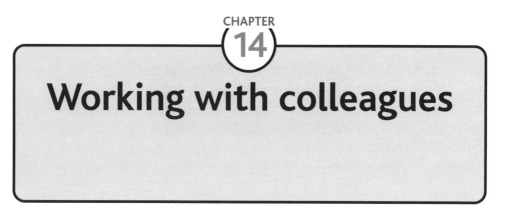

Working with colleagues

This first chapter in Part 4 concentrates on the other people you work with inside your organisation, starting with a summary of some of the most common job roles and responsibilities which exist in PCE other than teachers. Understanding the variety of personalities you may encounter within your organisation is approached through the theme of personality traits next in the chapter. We look at how the different personalities can interact positively and negatively with each other in interesting and challenging ways, and the chapter closes by considering how to build an effective team. By the end of the chapter, surviving working with your colleagues should become less of a challenge.

Who are your colleagues?

The diversity of PCE includes a wide range of jobs, and given the variety of learning sites at which provision operates, it is difficult to generalise about the type of colleagues you will be working with. At one end of the scale you may be part of a department in a large further education college. Over 100 teaching staff may be employed by that department, 60 of whom are full-time, and your immediate circle of teaching and non-teaching colleagues could be 50 or more in size. At the other end of the scale, as a part-time aromatherapy, literacy or French teacher, who teaches only during the evening in community venues for 2–3 hours per week and at the most 30 weeks of the year, your immediate colleagues may be the caretaker, the person teaching in the room next door, and the security person or key holder! Certain departments or functions do tend to be present in all but the smallest organisations in PCE and most teachers will have contact with them. Brief descriptions of some of those most common functions follow.

Student support

Exactly what is part of student support will vary from one organisation to another, but this area of work is generally focused on providing individual students and groups of students with assistance related to their learning. Generally the assistance helps students to join, stay on and achieve in learning programmes, and staff providing student support are extremely important in making the difference between achievement and underachievement in many cases. They often work directly with the teaching team, so can be some of the closest colleagues you will have.

Student support involves:

- providing specialist support staff to work directly (often one-to-one) with students in and outside their sessions, according to the particular needs of those students;
- organising and providing advice and guidance services for prospective, current and past students including course information, careers advice, counselling and pastoral care;
- monitoring and supporting attendance by, and progress of, students on programmes;
- early identification of, and support for, students who may be 'at risk' in various ways of dropping out;
- providing and co-ordinating facilities for students to make use of enrichment activities and social facilities;
- providing information about and referral to other organisations, programmes and staff who can assist students when in difficulty.

Learning resources and information/study skills

Another important group of staff organise, monitor the use of and make available the learning resources of the organisation for students and staff. This normally includes information professionals in the library or learning resource centre, who provide training and support in the use of learning resources, information and study skills in addition to library lending services.

Their work generally involves:

- managing and operating the library desk lending system for books and other loan items;
- training staff and students in library use, study skills, information skills and specialist electronic services;
- identifying and locating resources for staff in requested areas;
- managing bookings for computers and Internet facilities, and overseeing facilities such as virtual learning environments;

- maintaining a suitable study environment for students in learning resource centres;
- working with staff to create learning resources for their teaching.

Technical support, admin and facilities

Without this group of staff, organisations would quickly grind to a halt, irrespective of the quality of the teachers. Without receptionists, technicians, caretakers, canteen staff, security and maintenance the buildings would be cold, closed and dirty, and the students hungry, uncomfortable and untidy. With e-learning in particular, technical support is as important as the content and style of the learning programmes. If you can't get online or your projector doesn't work, you can't e-learn. At their best, these staff can provide creative and essential contributions to the teaching and learning of any organisation.

THINKING POINT

Not the teacher

What is likely to be the common factor in the answers to all these questions?

- When prospective students contact your organisation, who is likely to be the first person they speak to?

- As a student arrives at your organisation for the first time, what is going to make the initial impression on them?

- If a student has a problem with a computer in the learning resources centre, who will be available to help?

- If a student isn't sure where their class is, who will tell them?

- When a student passes their qualification, who gets the certificate to them?

The answer to all these questions is almost certainly 'not the teacher'. Does that help you to realise how important everyone else in the organisation other than teachers actually is?

Personality traits

As we have indicated throughout the book, PCE works with a great range and diversity of students. It also employs an almost equally diverse body of staff, ranging from conventionally 'academic' trained professional teachers to vocational specialists who have moved from industry to teaching, past students who move into teaching after being students and people who are working in other jobs while teaching part-time. Add to that the range of people who work in the sector who are not teaching but doing other jobs within teaching organisations and you get an interesting mixture.

We looked at group dynamics in Chapter 12 as one way of understanding how different people interact and how you can manage that as a teacher. When it comes to the teachers, group dynamics is equally important, and you could use that understanding when working with other teachers. Another way is to consider the personality traits of any group of staff or their individual personality differences. Personality types and how they work together are a major concern in organisational and management development, but it is a field in which it is easy to become buried under test results, questionnaires, analysis and complications. My example is an approach to personality which I feel is accessible and clear, but based on sound theory.

The Five Factor Model of Personality

In the field of personality types, the Five Factor Model, as it is called, has recently found a wide range of admirers. Its major proponents are McRae and Costa (1996), who argue that the factors are not fixed points but points on a scale, with many people falling between the extremes. Your place on the scale is believed to stay stable through much of adult life, so it should be possible to make use of this approach to understand behaviour over an extended period of time.

The five factors are as follows:

1 Extraversion

Extraverts tend to be more physically and verbally active, whereas introverts are independent, reserved, steady and like being alone. The person in the middle of the dimension likes a mix between social situations and solitude. Extraverts are adventurous, assertive, frank, sociable and talkative. Introverts are quiet, reserved, shy and unsociable.

Impact in the workplace   Extraverts are felt to be communicative, visioning and ready to engage in interpersonal relations, qualities which should be useful in leaders or potential leaders. Introverts may function effectively within a supportive group, but could find regular face-to-face contact with students and staff challenging. A large number of either in a workplace would be problematic.

2 Agreeableness

Agreeable personalities tend to be good-natured, caring, sympathetic and forgiving. Disagreeable people are indifferent, self-centred, jealous and rude.

Impact in the workplace   If your workplace was full of people who are on the disagreeable end of the scale (particularly if they are managers), this would have a highly negative impact, as they would be likely to pressure and coerce others. Agreeable traits would contribute to an emotionally positive environment and could impact significantly in terms of teamwork and flexibility or 'give and take'.

3 Conscientiousness

The conscientious person is focused, reliable, well-organised, self-disciplined and careful. The slacker is impulsive, unreliable, easy to put off and lacks organisation.

Impact in the workplace   The conscientious are in many ways, as the name suggests, the 'conscience' of the organisation, who are likely to promote ethics and values while putting in consistent effort and being ready to work with others. Slackers are probably the biggest burden any organisation carries.

4 Neuroticism

Those with a tendency towards neuroticism are worried, temperamental, insecure and prone to sadness. Emotionally stable personalities are calm, stable and relaxed.

Impact on the workplace   Stress in the workplace can breed neuroticism and can lead those who are not generally nervous into bouts of worrying, hesitance and disengagement from their work. Neurotics can become detached and distant from their co-workers and their workplace. Promoting emotional stability, the other end of this scale, should be a central concern of all workplaces and can strongly foster teamwork, productivity and efficiency.

5 Openness

People with high openness have broader interests and are complex, liberal, creative and curious. Those who are more closed tend to be conventional, uncreative, have narrow interests and avoid new experiences.

Impact on the workplace   Those who are open will be the thinkers, visioners and creative forces at work but will also be sensitive to the internal and external context they are working in. The closed thinkers may well see openness as dangerous and difficult to manage so can be troubled by 'too much' openness.

Using the five factors

When you look at these descriptions, you will naturally start rating yourself and the people you work with and know. The results you come up with will inevitably be affected by how honest you are and how much you are prepared to admit some of your less attractive personality traits. The simple activity which follows will help you identify where you and selected others fit on the Five Factor Model.

THINKING POINT

The Five Factor Quiz – what are you like?

- Use your initials and mark where you think you are on the matrix for each personality trait, working through all five factors.

- Join the points together into a continuous line to see your profile.

- Add ratings for at least two other people in your organisation, one of whom should be the senior manager.

Table 14.1 The Five Factor Quiz – what are you like?

Factor	Rating							Factor
	3	2	1	0	1	2	3	
Extraversion								Introversion
Agreeableness								Disagreeableness
Emotional stability								Neuroticism
Conscientiousness								Slackness
Openness								Closed

adapted from McRae and Costa

The overall profile will give you some significant insights into the mix of personalities in your organisation and can be really revealing if you profile all of your team. The factors on the left are generally considered to be more positive than those on the right, but that doesn't necessarily mean a workplace full of people with profiles along the left-hand side will necessarily be the most productive and effective. It is possible to get a good indication of the balance of personalities in your team from a profiling exercise such as this. There are no hard and fast rules about which personality traits must be mixed together, so we strongly advise using such profiles as indicators only.

From personalities to a working team

Using the matrix, you can identify the personality traits of as many of your working colleagues as you wish. If you are an open, conscientious, agreeable and emotionally stable extrovert who is surrounded by closed, disorganised, disagreeable and neurotic introverts, you are probably somewhat scared. Equally, if you were surrounded by people who all had the same personality traits as you, would that work? The key challenge for you and your organisation is to make the best use of the different personality types available to produce a balanced team. Teams can still work effectively despite containing apparently incompatible personalities, just as teams can be ineffective despite appearing to have the perfect blend of personalities. The crucial message is that

effective teamwork is at the centre of any successful organisation.

A major research project into teamworking in the UK National Health Service operated over a three-year period and involved 400 teams, 7,000 NHS personnel and a 'large number' of NHS clients. The report on this research, from the Aston Centre for Health Service Organisation Research (2000) makes some significant points about teamwork. Mohrman and Cohen's definition of a team (1995: 3) is used, which describes it as:

> a group of individuals who work together to produce products or deliver services for which they are mutually accountable. Team members share goals and are mutually held accountable for meeting them, they are interdependent in their accomplishment, and they affect the results through their interactions with one another. Because the team is held collectively accountable, the work of integrating with one another is included among the responsibilities of each member.

This model of teamwork is highly relevant to PCE, and the conclusions of the research emphasise a number of characteristics of effectively functioning teams. I have used those characteristics to inform my own 'Dream team checklist'.

Dream team checklist

Teams work effectively when:

- providing a high-quality service is the key motivating factor;
- innovation is encouraged;
- people from different disciplines have opportunities to work together;
- objectives are clear;
- participation by team members is high;
- meetings and communication are regular and clear.

The benefits for the team, its members and the organisation include:

- clearer leadership, more effective team processes;
- innovation and improvements in the quality of service;

- reduced stress for team members;
- wider benefits for all including increased morale, confidence and autonomy.

STRATEGY FOR SURVIVAL

Picking your dream team

Thinking back on the personality traits of the people in your organisation and considering the checklist above, use this activity to develop your 'dream team'. Bear in mind you probably don't have the power to change the personalities, so this is about using teamwork to overcome differences and accentuate positives.

- Identify two ways in which your team is working effectively and two in which it is not.

- Identify two ways in which the organisation as a team is working effectively and two in which it is not.

- Decide on an area where you believe you have some capacity to change the situation for the better.

- Write down two actions you will take to improve teamworking over the next month.

- Get teamworking!

- Make sure you check in a month to see how it worked out.

References

Aston Centre for Health Service Organisation Research (2000) *Healthcare Team Effectiveness Project.* Birmingham: Aston University

McRae, P. R. and Costa, P. T. (1996) Toward a new generation of personality theories: theoretical contexts for the Five-Factor model, in J. S. Wiggins (ed.) *The Five-factor Model of Personality. Theoretical Perspectives.* New York: Guilford Press

Mohrman, S. A., Cohen, S. G. and Mohrman, A. M. Jr (1995) *Designing Team-based Organisations.* San Francisco: Jossey-Bass

Working under pressure and managing conflict

This chapter takes a look at two related areas which teachers in PCE have often said they are least prepared for: a workload and working situation which puts them under intense pressure, and managing conflict which may arise outside the classroom. I start by explaining what I call the 'three Ps': paper pressure, people pressure and personal pressure. The chapter then emphasises how important it is to learn to stay calm and be positive, remembering there is more to life than work alone. Focused advice on ways of prioritising and managing time follows, and then an introduction to what can cause conflict, and some basic techniques for managing conflict situations.

Paper pressure, people pressure and personal pressure

Most of the aspects of pressure fall under the three Ps and you need to remember they are not necessarily always negative types of pressure.

Paper pressure

We may be in an electronic age, but the mountain of paper which can pile up on a teacher's desk during just one week is quite staggering at times. Add to this the 'electronic paper' (that is the items which arrive in your inbox for example rather than as hard copy) and you really do have paper pressure. Even deciding whether to print the electronic paper adds further pressure. A typical selection could include:

- paper for your teaching – documentation directly related to your teaching (e.g. schemes of work, session plans, handouts, transparencies, assessment tasks, assignment briefs, etc.);
- paper for your students – student support publications/documentation (e.g. organisational handbooks for your course, from other departments, promoting services for students);

- paper for your learning programmes – the syllabus or curriculum you are working with (e.g. a typical Advanced Vocational Certificate of Education specification document is a 3-megabyte download from the examination board and runs to 281 pages);
- paper from inside – internal communications (e.g. notes/memos from colleagues, staff circulars, minutes of meetings, policies, procedures);
- paper from outside – external communications (e.g. awarding body communications, reports, policy documents, notifications of meetings, staff development).

This does not even include other important paper pressures, such as marking student work or reading, research or investigation you may wish to carry out. Paper pressure is so intense that we shall deal with it in more detail in Chapter 18.

People pressure

People pressure is about the feelings, issues and complications which can arise when you are interacting with or responding to other people, sometimes out of choice, but not always. The people who have been significant contributors to your particular paper mountain can often be part of the pressure, but they are by no means the only people involved. At least with paper pressure you can find a quiet (or at least quieter) corner to read all the paper. But with people pressure you often need to sort it out face to face. The electronic age has made email contact much more common, but there are even people pressures associated with electronic communication, as there tends to be an inbuilt expectation of a rapid response. People pressure can come from:

- students who wish to be seen outside teaching/tutorial time;
- colleagues wishing to work collaboratively with you on something of mutual interest;
- external enquiries, liaison and contacts such as telephone calls, being present at publicity or recruitment events;
- managers who expect you to be available to see them at any time;
- sudden unexpected situations with any of the above.

Personal pressure

Personal pressure is about how you as a person receive, process and deal with all of the pressures involved in your life and work. Essentially, you are the person at the heart of all of this, so you need to develop your own ways of dealing with it and recognising the impact on yourself, your colleagues, friends and family.

If you are working to help other people, knowing yourself well is crucial.

The earlier content on personality traits and group dynamics should help here, but pause briefly for this next Thinking Point, to reflect on how you personally recognise and manage pressure.

THINKING POINT

Recognising the three Ps

With a friend or colleague, make a list of the most persistent paper, people and personal pressures you face in your work as a teacher. Group them under the different types of headings if that helps. Try to answer these questions:

- What strategies for dealing with pressure do you use generally and how well do they work?

- Choosing one of the most persistent pressures, how effectively do you manage it?

- Do you find any one of the three Ps more difficult than the others?

- What other strategies can you try to reduce pressure?

Calm down! Be positive!

It has been argued that being able to stay calm and think positively can help with managing most problems and issues in life, and I would generally endorse that view. From thinkers and philosophers such as Gandhi and Carl Rogers, and from non-violent protests to therapeutic relationships, emphasis is given to what I would describe as 'active calmness'. This is not a state of passive acquiescence, but rather more positively charged calmness, which is a combination of relaxed self-awareness and positive thinking. How can we work to achieve active calmness when there are so many pressures surrounding us?

STRATEGY FOR SURVIVAL

Calm down

Relaxing in pressured situations is by definition difficult, as there are both physical (hormones released in stressful situations can make us feel we need to run away) and psychological (various reactions, ranging from being ill at ease to panic attacks) factors involved. However, it is possible to keep those feelings and reactions at bay. Some simple techniques to use are as follows:

- pause and count to ten – the age-old technique of stopping for a brief period of time and thinking before reacting. Gives pause for thought and can make a real difference.

- action replay – run through the pressures which are making you anxious and ask yourself, Are they really as bad as I thought they were?

- buffer zone – make sure you have activities (e.g. hobbies, friends and family, travel, reading novels) which are nothing to do with work to take you away from your pressure sources and give you a zone to learn to relax.

- fit for purpose – if you are unhealthy, unfit and run down, you will find keeping calm even more difficult. Find a simple starting point to making yourself more 'fit for purpose', such as taking breaks even if they are only five minutes long or walking more instead of using the car.

STRATEGY FOR SURVIVAL

Be positive

In terms of working with pressure, being positive is all about not getting weighed down by the pressures at every stage, and can also help what I have called being 'actively critical' earlier in the book. Much of this is about mindsets, but it is possible to move away from being negative if you are prepared to try to make some changes in the way you think about pressures. You can remain positive by:

- challenging demanding musts, shoulds, have tos, oughts and got tos: just stop and question some of those immediate and perhaps understandable negative thoughts and responses. Is the latest deadline as real as my head is telling me? Is my thinking about the deadline helpful or stress-inducing? Where is my thinking getting me?

- Challenging 'awfulising' beliefs: is it really going to be awful if I don't achieve the deadline or goal? Will it really be the end of the world? Am I turning a 'life hassle' into a 'life horror'? Am I making a mountain out of a molehill?

- Challenging 'I can't stand it-itus': will I really fall apart and not be able to stand the outcome? Surely I'm living proof that I've survived not reaching deadlines on previous occasions?

- Challenging global ratings of self or others: is it fair to rate myself (or others) globally as a total failure if I've failed to accomplish one task?

Using this approach to positive thinking means that thoughts like
'If I don't make that deadline it will be awful and I'll be a failure'
become
'If I failed to reach the deadline on this occasion, I just failed to reach the deadline – that's all. I have done my best and I will do my best with the next deadline' (adapted from Clow and Palmer 2004).

Prioritising and managing time

Having now achieved 'active calm' and established positive thoughts, not very much is going to change if your workload is so high that you still have far more to do than can possibly be done in the time you have available to do it. Not only that, overwork is guaranteed to make your feelings of calm rapidly disappear. There are some simple routines and approaches to managing your time which can genuinely make a difference, but there is one key requirement, without which not much will change.

You need to master the art of saying 'no'.

This does not mean being the 'awkward squad' and it does not mean you are not committed to your job and your students. It means you wish to operate in a positive, effective and efficient manner and that you are prepared to firmly and assertively explain why you can't always do everything. Don't forget that stress reduces your performance so it is not in anyone's interest for you to work 25 hours a day.

STRATEGY FOR SURVIVAL

Bin it!

This can be a really helpful way of prioritising and is based on taking limited risks with what you decide to prioritise. You need to be brave and to pause and think about work before you get started on it.

- As work comes in, create three piles: the 'do it', 'leave it' and 'bin it' piles. (Even if the work isn't on paper, writing the task down and putting it on one of these piles helps.)

- Don't actually bin anything at this stage.

- Do the 'do it' tasks first, then the 'leave it' tasks.

- The first few times, don't do the 'bin it' tasks for a short time and see whether they return to haunt you. If not, simply don't do the 'bin it' tasks.

- If you feel uncomfortable with binning it, experiment with moving items from the 'leave it' and 'bin it' piles and see what happens.

Time management matrix

A more gentle and perhaps less risky way of planning your time is what tends to be called a 'time management matrix'. Stephen Covey (1990) produced such a tool and the overall idea is to place items in the matrix based on how

	Urgent	Not urgent
Important	**Quadrant 1** Crises Pressing problems Deadlines	**Quadrant 2** Exploiting new opportunities Building relationships Planning Reviewing Recreation
Not important	**Quadrant 3** Interruptions Some phone calls/emails Some meetings	**Quadrant 4** Trivia Some phone calls/emails Some meetings Waste of time Task avoidance

Figure 15.1 Time management matrix

'important' or 'not important' they are on one dimension, and how 'urgent' or 'not urgent' they are along the other. Figure 15.1 illustrates the four quadrants of the matrix and suggests some of the items which may be placed in each quadrant.

Covey (1990: 3) argues: 'Quadrant 2 is the heart of effective personal management. It deals with things that are not urgent, but are important.' By planning to spend more time in Quadrant 2, we can take another look at workload and priorities and create solutions that, over time, reduce the quantity and urgency of items typically found in Quadrants 1 and 3.

STRATEGY FOR SURVIVAL

Reloading the matrix

- Complete your own version of the time management matrix at the same time as one other person completes their own.

- Select two items from Quadrant 2 and agree with your partner that you will give them more time over the next two weeks. This is your time management contract.

- Get together again in two weeks (time permitting, of course) and honour the contract. Having to report on your changes to someone else reduces the chance of you finding excuses not to do it.

Understanding conflict and managing conflict situations

John Crawley, who has written extensively on conflict management, defines conflict as 'a manifestation of differences working against one another' (Crawley 1992: 10). He goes on to argue that conflicts can 'explode' and the components which make them explosive are:

- ingredients – the differences which are present between people including age, gender, values, beliefs, status and behaviours;
- combinations and conditions – the contacts between people and the structures and environment in which they live and work;
- the spark – the clash of differences;
- the burning fuse – circumstances and feelings which can slowly ignite the conflict such as defensiveness, power games and inability to find a resolution;
- the explosion – a dramatic, violent exchange which affects the people nearby as well as those directly involved.

All of us have probably experienced 'explosive' conflicts, either at work or at home, and resolving them once they have become explosive can be exceptionally difficult and can involve emotional, material and financial costs. There are therefore huge gains to be made by reducing and managing conflict.

Managing conflict effectively promotes positive personal interactions, but can also be efficient and cost-effective.

Co-operative (win/win) conflict

How then can we avoid explosions of conflict? 'Conflicts need not always turn out this way. Constructive conflict management will enable you to transform the interaction' (Crawley 1992: 10). This approach sees conflict as a mutual problem to be solved by collaborative effort, where all parties have something to gain. This recognises all parties' interests as legitimate and seeks a solution which is responsive to the needs of all. The approach is more concerned with looking for ways forward, solving problems and creating more effective working relationships, rather than settling arguments about right and wrong, or attributing blame.

Managing conflict using this problem-solving style means you need to:

- see big problems as a series of smaller problems and tackle them a little at a time;
- evaluate the impact of possible solutions as you explore them;
- collect background information about the problem and the expectations and needs of all involved;

- get people to say how they see things, how they feel and what they want rather than labelling or blaming;
- get some agreement about action and keep on track with the action;
- take it steadily, e.g. do not rush into solutions;
- keep working even when things are getting tough.

Conflict situations

Three brief descriptions follow of potentially explosive conflict situations which you may come across outside the classroom. Think about how you could stop these happening using some of the approaches I have presented so far. Some suggestions will appear at the end of the section.

Feedback from the boss

Your immediate boss has recently changed and the new person rarely gives you positive feedback about your work, tending to pick out and emphasise small problems. He has interrupted you in meetings and postponed supervision sessions with you, and your overall impression is that your work is not valued highly.

Chalk and cheese

Two of your colleagues, who have spaces in the office you all share with six other staff, just do not get on with each other. One has been working for the organisation for 22 years and is 46, and the other for just six months and is 23. They have different views about many things, but both teach the same subject. When working together they regularly make negative comments about each other and they have been heard having heated discussions out in the corridor by the office, which usually end with one or the other stomping off aggrieved.

Team not working

A group of eight staff who work together have not gelled as a team, despite all working effectively as individuals in their own roles. When the group comes together, a tense atmosphere exists, and when they need to work co-operatively to implement a new initiative, progress is slow and uncomfortable. When they meet others in the organisation they tend to make negative comments about other members of the team.

THINKING POINT

Avoiding explosions

All of these situations are 'smouldering' and we want to stop them sparking into explosive conflict. Here are some strategies which could work. Match the strategies to the situations you think they could work in.

- Bring in others as mediators to work with the people in conflict. Take care about who is approached.

- Encourage the parties to the conflict to come together in groups and give them a chance to talk.

- Make positive use of time with your boss, be assertive and clarify expectations and understandings. Do you both know clearly what the other expects?

- Respond positively to challenges by being 'actively calm'.

- Get information quickly about differences between parties in a conflict to clarify what is going on.

- Ensure everyone is listened to but encourage them to listen as well.

- Look for small improvements which all can accept to move forward.

Making these adjustments can have a major impact on reducing conflict.

References

Clow, A. and Palmer, S. (2004) *The Stress Test.* London: British Broadcasting Company

Covey, S. (1990) *The Seven Habits of Highly Effective People.* New York: Simon & Schuster

Crawley, J. (1992) *Constructive Conflict Management – Managing to Make a Difference.* London: Nicholas Brealey Publishers

Are you teaching in a learning organisation?

This chapter starts by considering just what a learning organisation is and how it fits into our knowledge age and the world of PCE. Checking how your organisation rates as a learning organisation follows, together with some ideas about organisational culture and the way it can affect the day-to-day business of teaching and learning. The chapter concludes with a consideration of how power can operate in the smallest or the largest organisations, and some strategies for keeping that power on your side.

Learning organisations in the knowledge age

Much has been written and said on learning organisations, but just how much this is an ideal notion of an organisation and how much it is a reality can sometimes be difficult to judge. When organisations are operating in a climate of pressure and results are important, operating as a learning organisation could be seen to be of very much secondary importance, and even something of a luxury. In a rapidly changing, technologically sophisticated world, operating as a learning organisation is not so much a luxury as a necessity. Peter Senge has been influential in this area. His view is that learning organisations are

> organisations where people continually expand their capacity to create the results they truly desire, where new and expansive patterns of thinking are nurtured, where collective aspiration is set free, and where people are continually learning to see the whole together.
>
> (Senge 1990: 3)

This vision could be seen as somewhat idealistic, but the emphasis on the value of teamwork and learning together is really important. Charles Handy has a typically clear and accessible contribution to this theme, which is the learning organisation can mean two things – it can mean an organisation which learns and/or an organisation which encourages learning in its people. It should mean both.

(Handy 1995: 179)

Any organisation which does not pay careful attention to the processes and interactions between its workers and see them as a developing and learning team is not just out of date, it is foolish. Working towards common goals which at least in part overlap with individual goals is essential for most of us, whether we are building cars, helping our workmates, nursing the elderly or teaching. The gains and positive benefits of working together in a shared atmosphere of learning are economic, social and personal, and after all

if an organisation which has teaching as its core business cannot try to be a learning organisation, we may as well all give up and go home.

THINKING POINT

Is yours a learning organisation?
The statements in Table 16.1 reflect current thinking on the characteristics of a learning organisation. Rate your organisation against each statement from 1 to 4 (1 is low and 4 is high).

Table 16.1 Is yours a learning organisation?

Organisational area	Rating (1–4)
Organisational dynamics	
We are encouraged to manage our own learning and development	
A positive listening and feedback environment exists	
Training is available in how to learn	
Teams and individuals use the wheel of learning to reflect and act on their learning	
Teachers are supported to take a strategic approach	
The organisation's approach to change and development	
Senior managers accept the idea of a learning organisation	
There is a climate which supports the idea of learning	
We learn from our weaknesses and our achievements	
Opportunities to learn are part of day-to-day business	
There is a flat management structure which promotes communication and learning at all levels	

Table 16.1 (continued)

Organisational area	Rating (1–4)
Empowerment of people	
The workforce is empowered to work and learn	
Authority is delegated and decentralised	
Managers have a facilitative, mentoring approach	
We share with other organisations to improve our service and theirs	
We participate in joint learning events with other relevant PCE stakeholders	
Managing knowledge	
We benchmark our best practices against others and seek to learn from them	
Training and support is available for staff in innovation and creative thinking	
Trialling and evaluating new areas of work is embedded in our practice	
We and others are able to make use of our accumulated knowledge in our field	
We share that knowledge systematically and on an ongoing basis with others	
Technological support	
Our uses of technology clearly benefit our key purpose	
Staff and students have ready access to the Internet and other learning technology	
Learning technology is embedded in our practice	
We make use of e-learning within our curriculum	
We make use of technology to support our evaluation and development systems	
Total score (out of 100)	

The maximum score here is 100. If you scored 40 or below, your organisation is in trouble.

Organisational culture

Organizational culture is the set of, often unconsciously held, beliefs, ideas, knowledge and values which shape the way things happen and makes some courses of action unthinkable. An organization's culture therefore determines, to a large extent, its capacity for solving problems. (Bate 1994: 224)

Organisational culture is manifested almost as soon as you get anywhere near any organisation and can have a major impact not just on whether the organisation is a learning organisation but on all aspects of what the organisation does and stands for. It is not of course the only thing which affects how an organisation works, as where you are situated geographically, the resources you have at your disposal, your relative size and financial position, to name a few, all have an impact. Changing organisational culture can be enormously difficult however, partly because it tends to start at the top of the organisation and partly because we are not in an environment which provides much time and space for thinking about organisational culture and how to change or improve it.

THINKING POINT

The 'walk-about audit' – testing the organisational culture

Try a 'walk-about audit' where you just walk around any organisation involved in PCE. What do these comments from walk-about audits tell you about the culture of the organisations involved?

- You walk in the gates of your local college. What you see first is a mixture of older and newer buildings. They all appear well looked after and the site is really clean, with flowerbeds providing splashes of colour to greet you. Along the drive and footpaths are well-positioned pieces of student work, including sculptures, displays and murals. You can find your way to reception easily.

- You arrive for an evening class in a small rural learning centre. It's midwinter outside, but a warm coffee bar is sited just as you go in and you join a small group of students who are already seated chatting before starting their classes. The centre administrator is welcoming all arrivals and passing round copies of next year's prospectus of classes and a leaflet on some new computer training.

- You arrive at one of the campuses of a college you are considering attending full-time. The buildings are run down and finding the right building is extremely hard, as there are either no signs or they are broken. To get into the building, you have to go through a group of people smoking outside the door and when you get inside there is no receptionist and no clear signs showing where to go. You wait at reception for several minutes before anyone asks you what you want, and then wait 20 minutes to see someone.

Isn't that first impression powerful? We discussed the more general aspects of working with colleagues in Chapter 14, but just ask yourself the question,

Where would you rather learn or work out of the examples above? The examples show well that

> **organisational culture is physically invisible, but you will see its effects everywhere.**

If culture is that pervasive, what can we do to change or improve it? Because organisational culture is mainly a shared concept, people can sometimes feel their capacity to make any change is limited, and a feeling of helplessness can result.

> Any one member of an organisation can influence and change the culture of that organisation by making 'choices for change'.

STRATEGY FOR SURVIVAL

Choices for change

When you are under pressure, you may feel it is difficult to get involved in changing the culture of your organisation. You've done the learning organisation rating and the organisation does badly. There are ways to get involved in trying to change negative aspects of the organisation's culture, but you must wholeheartedly engage with the positive aspects. Here are some suggestions of 'choices for change' you could make:

- The Internet café in your organisation is a much more pleasant place to meet colleagues and actually relax than the general canteen. Arrange to have a meeting with your team manager there and ask them to think about how they feel it compares with the canteen.

- You have found a really good web site, which you think is worth everyone in your subject team using. Organise a lunchtime demo of the site and provide coffee and cakes to give your team a hands-on taste of the web site.

- Sit in your reception area and watch people arriving for appointments or as visitors. How long do they have to wait, how are they dealt with, and how comfortable/confident do they look? Make some notes and report back on it to your next departmental meeting, asking for comments.

- Do a 'walk-about audit' – take a digital camera out around your site, capturing the best and worst bits. Show both to your boss, your colleagues and your students and ask them what they can do to make things better.

These are all very small steps, but

> you can help change to happen, so grasp the opportunity.

Power and influence

As a teacher in an organisation, whether a small or large one, you both have power and are affected by power in a variety of ways. Organisations, their cultures, systems and processes, and the way they develop, can change dramatically depending on the power relationships which operate in those organisations. According to Paton (1994: 191) 'anyone who must regularly attempt to get things done with and through other people has the problem of generating agreement, or perhaps just consent, or at least compliance with regards to what must be done, how, when and on what terms'. In doing that, those people will 'make use of whatever resources or means are available, and seem appropriate' (Paton: 191). One of the most common resources used is power, and Paton describes four types.

Position power

This is the power which comes from a person's formal position in an organisation. The higher or more senior your position in an organisation, the more you are likely to exercise a greater degree of position power. Position power tends to attract status and respect, sometimes irrespective of how it is used. If you have position power in your organisation, you can generally use it in most situations, relative to that position in the organisation. The most obvious example of position power would tend to be the boss or head of any organisation.

Expert power

This is power which is more to do with specialist knowledge, skills and understanding than with position in an organisation, and indeed can be a power which at times exerts influence way above the position of the person who holds it in the organisation. Someone who is a technical expert with computers, for instance, could exercise a high degree of expert power even if they do not hold a senior position. When the head of the organisation's computer breaks down, the technicians hold considerable expert power. Expert power is likely to exert influence in fewer situations than position power.

Dependence power

This is power which relates to how much the different people in an organisation rely or depend on others in the organisation. If someone depends on you for something particular in the organisation, you have dependence power. There is some overlap with expert power, but a relatively low level of expertise can still exercise dependence power. If you are a group of people whom others depend on (such as the security staff who lock and unlock premises), you may be able to exercise power which is greater than position power. The difference is you will almost certainly be able to do this in only a limited number of situations.

Personal power

This is about 'those abilities and qualities which enable some people to make the most of whatever other power resources they have' (Paton 1994: 193). Charm, sensitivity, anticipation and self-confidence may all give you personal power. Depending on how well you are able to exercise this particular type of power, you may be able to insulate yourself reasonably well from any conflict resulting from other forms of power. We all know people who appear to succeed whatever the circumstances. They have personal power.

These are not the only ways in which power operates, and you may at times feel you have none of those types of power. The key question to constantly ask is:

How can I use whatever combinations of power are available to the benefit of the students I am teaching?

Approaches to recognising and working with the power in your organisation are similar to those suggested in Chapter 15. Working through this Thinking Point will help you to more fully recognise the power relationships and responsibilities in your organisation.

THINKING POINT

Who's got the power?
Look at the types of power described in this section and ask yourself:

● Who has the different types of power in my organisation and how do they use it?

● What power do I have in the organisation and how do I use it?

● What power do I have with my students and how do I use it?

STRATEGY FOR SURVIVAL

Power to the people
There will be many times that power inside and outside your organisation will affect your working life and by no means all will involve pain or disappointment. Power can be a positive and negative influence – the trick is to be able to predict in advance the positive or the negative aspects of power in your organisation. The more difficult part is to then avoid the negative,

or at least mitigate its effects, and ride the wave of the positive. Follow these golden rules and they should help:

- Make sure you are aware of who has power in your organisation and why.

- Observe how that power is exercised and how possible it may be to resist, counteract or avoid it.

- Be prepared with strategies to take advantage of opportunities which power may present.

- Do not use any power you may have to exploit others.

- You have more power than you may think with your students. Use it wisely.

References

Bate, P. (1994) Organizational culture, in Armson, R. and Paton, R. (eds) *Organisations – Cases, issues, concepts.* 2nd edition. London: Paul Chapman Publishing

Paton, R. (1994) Power in organizations, in Armson, R. and Paton, R. (eds) *Organisations – Cases, issues, concepts.* 2nd edition. London: Paul Chapman Publishing

Senge, P. M. (1990) *The Fifth Discipline. The art and practice of the learning organization.* London: Random House

Handy, C. (1995) *The Age of Unreason.* London: Arrow

PART 5

Moving out of the deep end

Reality check . . . how's it going?

This chapter is aimed at providing you with a reality check for your teaching career to date, which I am confident will signal that you have now moved out of the 'deep end' and are growing in confidence that you will never return to its troubled waters. You will pause, reflect and ask yourself some crunch questions about how you feel, where you're going, and where you plan to be in the next year or two.

The chapter begins by offering you the chance to reflect on your teaching experiences to date and how you have been managing them so far, using themes covered in earlier parts of the book. You will use these reflections to 'future gaze' about how your growing mastery could enhance your career prospects in PCE, and what to consider when career opportunities arise. The chapter closes with a brief consideration of the idea of the 'professional' in PCE, and the chance for you to ask yourself just how professional you feel at this stage of your career.

Out of the deep end?

At the start of the book, I explained my goal as being to help you survive and develop as an effective, confident, committed and reflective teacher. If you have been able to move some distance towards that goal, that is surely a cause for celebration. Although this book provides strategies to help you survive, you should by now have realised that developing your teaching to its full potential involves much more. What I also said right at the start of the book is that at some stage, and if you're both lucky and good at your job, you will often help to change someone else's world and life for the better. It's a big job, isn't it? Just don't lose sight of this key message:

Being a teacher in PCE should be about more than just surviving.

When a job has such elevated goals, regularly asking yourself 'How am I doing?' is not just sensible but essential. It can also help give you a sense of perspective, particularly if you share your thoughts with others who are ready to listen.

Checking back

A quick review of the chapter headings or thinking points in the book will remind you of the breadth and range of tasks, issues and activities a teacher in PCE is expected to cope with. However pressured and busy you have been, you will regularly have been reflecting on what has gone well and what has not, as all teachers do. The chances are you will also have received considerable informal and formal feedback on your teaching and performance from others, as this is very much part of the scene in PCE. That feedback will probably have been based on standards, formal requirements or workplace expectations and may well have not covered some of the most important questions. Take some time out now to work through the deep end reality check, which I hope will raise useful questions, some of which have not yet been asked in this book.

THINKING POINT

Deep end reality check

Working through the reality check as a task with other people will be helpful, although they will need to be those whom you work closely with. It can be a very effective team-building activity or peer review tool. With each question, ask yourself two things. 'How do I think I'm doing?' and 'How do others think I'm doing?'. How you proceed is something you can decide for yourself, but you may wish to consider:

- grouping the statements and working on them over more than one session;

- putting your reflections on each statement down on paper (or word-processing them) as paragraphs, key words, mind maps, flow charts or images;

- rating each statement according to your degree of confidence in that area of your work, using 'very confident', 'confident', 'fairly confident' and 'lacking confidence';

- rating each answer numerically from high to low.

Reality check question 1   How do you think you are . . . ?
Reality check question 2   How do others think you are . . . ?

- coping overall with the challenges of teaching in PCE

- finding your work rewarding, fun and enjoyable

- feeling energetic, enthusiastic and resilient

- changing lives and creating a civil society

- riding the rollercoaster of PCE through the wheel of learning

---

- pushing the limits and being actively critical

- developing your specialist subject and getting mentored

- working effectively and inclusively with your students

- keeping the 'learning' in e-learning

- managing conflict and dealing with paper, people and personal pressures

- contributing to developing a learning organisation

- understanding and working with power

STRATEGY FOR SURVIVAL

Stand up but share the burden

Dealing with the types of problems which could occur from such a reality check is outside the scope of a book of this nature, but there are key pieces of advice I can give you:

- Make sure you receive both 'official' and 'unofficial' supervision, mentoring and support within your working situation. Trying to solve problems and build on your strengths should not be your job alone.

- Use the confidence from areas in which you feel you do well to draw up your confidence in areas in which you feel less confident. Look for improvement in small steps.

- Be ready to argue a calm and effective case when you need to, and stand your ground.

Prospects, possibilities and opportunities

Just how career prospects develop in PCE is less clearly defined than other areas of education and this is partly due again to the size, scope and diversity of the sector. When you are working in a large FE college, with hundreds of staff, and you are on a permanent contract, teaching in a faculty team of 50, the routes you may take to development, promotion or advancement are reasonably clear (although not necessarily plentiful). If you are working as a part-time IT tutor in two learning centres, one in a company and one in a neighbourhood adult education centre, on a one-year temporary contract, where do you go from there? Lots of jobs are advertised and recruited through the conventional means, but many people progress in their careers as 'portfolio teachers', changing what they teach, where they work and who they work for on a regular basis, depending largely on supply and demand or their own preferences.

There are still large numbers of teachers who do not know whether they are going to get paid work until literally their first session. If enough students arrive or register, the class goes ahead. If not there is no work. Many staff are also employed on short-term contracts because of funding associated with short-term initiatives. Providing advice on career prospects in PCE is therefore not exactly a precise science!

Often, if an opportunity arises, there is a momentum associated with it, which can make decisions rushed and ill thought through. At times things come along and you can't say 'no' or you aren't given the choice to say 'no'. There is a saying, 'decide in haste – repent at leisure', and it is particularly true here. I would argue that injecting thinking time into your career decisions is sensible, and here are some ways you can do that.

What, where and when?

First, you know best, or you should do, which parts of your work you enjoy most and least, and probably which parts of the job you excel at and are not so good at. You also know how much you need to earn to make ends meet. When you make decisions about your future, make sure you ask yourself these questions before deciding:

- What do I enjoy most about the job I do, what am I best at, and what do I really need to earn to survive?

- Where do I most enjoy doing the job and feel most at home and at ease with my workmates and students?

- When might all of this change for the better or worse, and when should I do something about it?

Your answers can provide something of a health check on your current situation, but should certainly mean you approach any choices you are presented with from a more informed perspective.

Taking opportunities

Because of the intense environment of change PCE operates within, a somewhat volatile and at times almost frighteningly unpredictable world is created. Carl Rogers' thoughts from 1983 seem just as relevant now as they were when he wrote them:

> If there is one truth about modern man, it is that he lives in an environment that is *continually changing.*
> (Rogers 1983: 22)

Alongside ongoing and rapid change, opportunities can often be presented for those who are ready, willing and able to make the most of them. The difficulty with opportunity is that it often contains positive and negative components. If you say 'yes' to those extra paid teaching hours, will you still be able to prepare your teaching as fully as you do now? If you take on that co-ordinating role without any extra pay, is it really likely to lead to better-paid work in the future? In my experience, certain types of opportunities will probably arise when you are working in PCE. Is there such a thing as an opportunity you can't refuse? That's a difficult one to answer, but there are activities and opportunities which are genuinely useful, challenging and beneficial more often than they are not. Some of them can help to reawaken lost or hidden interests and abilities, and some can take you into new and exciting areas of experience and expertise.

Opportunities worth taking

Projects

Many projects each year contribute new developments, improvements and services, and most organisations in PCE get involved in them. They are often funded from sources outside the organisation and include government initiatives, European-funded work, curriculum development and a large number of quality improvement activities. I would suggest you get involved in projects for a number of reasons:

- They give you a chance to operate and think somewhat 'outside the box' of the regular confines of your day-to-day schedule.

- You contribute to investigating and evaluating real activities and issues generally aimed at improving learning for your students.

- You will work with colleagues from other organisations or teams and be able to 'showcase' your own work and share effort across a wider community.

- You may get opportunities to travel locally, nationally or internationally as part of the work.

- You will be likely to develop new understandings and skills which will be directly helpful to you and your students.

Research

Some projects involve a research component, but research which is organised, structured, rigorous and leads to outcomes such as published reports is another positive opportunity. It can involve working in partnership with a recognised agency such as the Learning and Skills Development Agency, or arise as part of professional development or links with other organisations, universities or publishers. In addition to the advantages associated with projects, research can:

- lead to recognised publications in your field;
- develop deeper understandings of aspects of your own and others' work;
- build your profile in your field within and outside your organisation.

Creating

Creating is of course often involved in the best projects and research. What we are arguing however is that there is something special about the process of creating items as part of your work, using your particular skills and experience, which needs to be preserved. This field of endeavour is often squeezed out of the normal range of day-to-day activity, but should not be. Creating can include developing learning materials and resources for your teaching; producing articles, web pages and web sites; scripting scenarios, plays, activities; building and making objects and artefacts. The particular benefits of creating are that it will:

- keep alive your specialised skills and interests;
- enliven your 'normal' teaching work;
- reveal skills and understanding to others which they never knew you had;
- almost certainly enhance your students' learning.

Externalling

Perhaps more mundane, but equally important, externalling is about using your particular expertise in a structured way to help others outside your immediate working situation to develop theirs. It can involve internal or external verification or moderation of learning programmes, working for quality assurance organisations, national awarding bodies and others, and its particular benefits include:

- using your specialist expertise to help others improve their quality;
- comparing what you see externally with your own work and using it to enhance quality;
- contributing to the pool of expertise in your field;
- some of the work is paid.

To inject a final note of appropriate reality into this section, please remember this:

Taking opportunities will always involve extra time and effort, but it is often worth it.

What is a professional?

By this stage of the book, the word 'professional' has been used on many occasions, and in general terms you will have your own understanding of what it means to be a professional, and in particular a 'professional teacher' or 'teaching professional'.

What do you think makes a professional teacher?
If you were listing the qualities and characteristics of a professional teacher in PCE, what would you come up with and why? Compare your results with at least one other person.

Professionalism in PCE

An authoritative text on PCE (Lea *et al.* 2003) draws on established writing in the field to examine some key issues about changing ideas of professionalism.

> Textbook definitions of 'professional' usually include a combination of the following characteristics: long training programmes in specialist knowledge; an ethic of altruism; autonomous work practices; the presence of a professional association.
>
> (Lea 2003: 61)

Randle and Brady (1997) present a view of professionalism which includes:

- the primary importance of student learning and the teaching process;
- maintaining loyalty to students and colleagues;
- expressing concerns for academic standards;
- recognition of teachers as experts;
- resources for education being made available on the basis of educational need;
- some elements of autonomy being essential;
- quality being assessed on the basis of inputs and process;
- maintaining a spirit of collegiality.

The high degree of individual and subject autonomy represented in these views is difficult to maintain in the current environment of PCE, where external and internal controls are a powerful influence. The widespread use of institutional targets and performance measures, coupled with systems and procedures aiming to improve quality, leaves little space for the autonomous teacher. Official statements suggesting teachers need to be 'fully prepared to deliver the agenda for post compulsory education and training in the early years of the third millennium' (FENTO 2001: 6) do not help reduce this impression.

Pathway to a new professionalism?

Teaching is worth more than just delivering someone else's agenda, although it should always be accountable. I shall suggest in Chapter 21 that a real opportunity now exists to define the professional ground of a teacher in PCE, but I start here with some practical reflections on your teaching journey so far.

Capable or extended professional?

Hoyle (1980) provides a useful view of professionalism for teachers and describes two types of professionalism, which are at different ends of a continuum; the 'restricted professional' and the 'extended professional'. While using the idea of a continuum is useful, I prefer a different term. Given the range of pressures you work under in PCE, it's highly likely that you move between the 'extended' and 'restricted' modes at different times and in different circumstances. The term 'restricted' downplays the essential and highly skilled aspects of working hard and concentrating on your students. Isn't this in itself a highly positive achievement, especially early in your teaching career? I will use the term 'capable professional' as I believe it to be much more suitable.

Capable professionals . . .

- work hard, preparing their lessons and caring about their students;
- limit their outlook and do not think beyond their classroom or organisation;
- do not consider the broader picture concerning the purposes of education as relevant to them;
- are basically concerned with the practical and not with the wider theoretical aspects of their profession.

Extended professionals

- seek to improve by learning from other teachers and professional development activities;
- constantly question and try to link theory to practice;
- are continually developing as teachers and placing their classroom work in a wider educational context.

THINKING POINT AND STRATEGY FOR SURVIVAL

Becoming an extended professional

Consider where you feel you are currently as a professional.

- Where between capable and extended would you see yourself most often?

- What helps or hinders your progress towards the extended role?

- What three steps can you take to move towards the extended side?

- What help will you have available from your organisation to do this?

References

Further Education National Training Organisation (2001) *Further Education Sector Workforce Development – Consultation Version.* London: FENTO

Hoyle, E. (1980) Professionalisation and deprofessionalisation in education, in Hoyle, E. and Megarry, J. (eds) *World Yearbook of Education 1980: professional development of teachers.* London: Kogan Page

Lea, J. (2003) Overview: the organization of post compulsory education, in Lea, J., Hayes, D., Armitage, A., Lomas, L. and Markless, S. *Working in Post Compulsory Education.* Maidenhead: Open University Press

Randle, K. and Brady, N. (1997a) Managerialism and professionalism in the 'Cinderella service'. *Journal of Vocational Education and Training* 49 (1) 121–139

Rogers, C. (1983) *Freedom to Learn in the 80s.* Ohio: Charles Merrill

18

Dealing with bureaucracy and inspection

This chapter begins with a reminder (as if you needed it!) of the scope of bureaucracy in PCE and how at times it can seem to overwhelm the sector and all who work in it. Despite often genuinely highlighting and promoting good practice, inspection is one of the key creators of the PCE paper mountain, and we consider why this is the case. Using manuals and guidelines for inspectors and examples of organisations in PCE which have demonstrated excellence in teaching and learning, the chapter then provides the 'shining light or burning out' guide to making inspection work for you. The chapter concludes by presenting thoughts on other, more creative approaches to developing and ensuring quality in teaching and learning, with the 'people not paper manifesto'.

The ultimate paper pressure

Paper pressure, as one of the three Ps of paper, people and personal pressure, has already been mentioned briefly in Chapter 15. Although this chapter is in many ways about reducing paper pressure and through it the other pressures, it would be a mistake to believe that teachers can manage without any bureaucracy or administration.

Inside every excellent teacher lives an excellent organiser and administrator.

Speed reading, summarising, planning and punctuality are just as important to the success of your teaching as imagination, inspiration and motivation. If you are assessing your students, you often need sophisticated skills of time management, judgement and clarity of explanation. Marking 30 assignments correctly and quickly enough to get them back to students in the time your student charter says you should is as much an achievement of organisation as of academic prowess. Necessary administration helping the wheel of learning to turn is one thing, but generating mountains of paper which bury it is another. We are in an age when you can spend 30 minutes on the Internet and book a round-the-world trip with accommodation and buy most of the clothes you wish to wear on the trip. Yet in PCE, the apparently simple task of enrolling one student on a part-time course lasting just 20 hours usually requires the completion of ten or more documents and the efforts of staff which can add up to hours of their time. It must be possible to do things better.

Things can only get better

The purpose of inspection is 'to make judgements about the quality of education and training, the standards that are achieved by students, to evaluate the effectiveness of resources and their impact on learning' (LSDA 2004: 1). This is reasonable enough. One of the key problems created, however, is the way in which inspection 'forces all practitioners to make *explicit* whatever may have been *implicit* before, i.e. if it cannot be seen it cannot be inspected' (Lea 2003: 77). A great deal of time is spent by a large number of teachers (and quality managers, administration staff and others) making sure that we have recognisable evidence of what we do, so that our peers, managers, inspectors and others are able to see it and use it when judging us and our organisations and comparing them with others. When inspectors have visited an organisation, one of the most frequent comments you hear from staff afterwards is 'I agree with what they said, and that's roughly what I would have expected'. At the extreme end of logic we could therefore argue that inspection can be an exercise in telling us what we already know. At the other end of the scale the obvious response would be, if an organisation already knew it had weaknesses in certain areas, why didn't it do something to change that before inspection? Perhaps a more telling question would be:

How do we balance the time spent providing evidence of quality with the need to ensure we make time for improving quality?

> ### THINKING POINT
>
> ***Prove it!***
> Reflect on your last week of work:
>
> - What has worked really well and why?
>
> - What has not worked well and why not?
>
> - What evidence of your practice during the week do you have?
>
> - How can that evidence help you make improvements?

Shining light or burning out?

Organisations which set the pace for PCE by achieving excellent results can be accorded beacon status and are funded to 'promote innovation and share their good practice with the sector' (LSC 2003: i). Those which do not do so well tend to be 'named and shamed', then provided with help to improve, sometimes from the beacon organisations. This culture of 'shining light' or 'burning out' is a tough one, so making the right choices about what you are doing regarding inspection is very important. Based on a number of publicly available documents and examples, here is my guide to help you and your organisation to be nearer to the 'shining light' than 'burning out'.

Quality assurance arrangements should:

- actively involve students and staff, and take account of what they say;

- be an integral part of day-to-day operations;

- show clearly how things do get better for students and staff;

- welcome suggestions for improvements to systems from staff and students;

- minimise the duplication of information and data and over-reliance on either paper or electronic forms;

- act as an early-warning mechanism to detect problems and help to solve them;

- inform curriculum planning, initial teacher training and continuous professional development (CPD);

- celebrate and share good practice;

- produce an accurate picture of the state of play in the organisation at that time.

If quality assurance in your organisation doesn't do these things, you need to do whatever you can to change it so that it does.

STRATEGY FOR SURVIVAL

Preparing for inspection

As an individual teacher preparing for inspection you need to:

- keep your course files (day-to-day teaching documentation) active, up to date and student-focused;

- ensure course reviews and evaluations are up to date, you have evidence of actions taken and you can relate them to benchmark data;

- be able to track what has been happening on your courses for the last three years, including recruitment, retention and achievement;

- ensure you have organised any other relevant information about your teaching (such as course team minutes and external verifier reports) and that you can follow through actions you have taken at every stage.

Observation of teaching

Observation of teaching sessions has grown commonplace over the last 5–10 years. As a new teacher you will almost certainly be observed on a number of occasions during your first year. You should also get the chance to observe others teaching. Being observed is a great opportunity to develop both your skills and understanding as a teacher and the overall quality of teaching and learning in an organisation. The process of carrying out a teaching observation needs to be handled with considerable sensitivity, even if you are informally sitting in on a colleague's teaching to get a feel for how they do it. I see teaching observation as a part of a learning process for teachers, and using it as a means of checking on staff is to be avoided at all costs.

Observers of other teachers should:

- undertake training in lesson observation and feedback, which involves shadowing other observers;
- work to agreed approaches regarding criteria used, how and when feedback will be covered, judgements and grades used and records completed.

When being observed you need to:

- plan the session to promote learning and attainment;
- demonstrate the capacity to differentiate tasks and activities to meet the needs of different students;
- monitor learning and participation for the duration of the session;
- provide students with detailed, constructive and evaluative feedback, which will help them progress;
- regularly self-evaluate sessions using a checklist, diary or other means.

Quality improvement which works

When organisations adopt the approaches this chapter has been advocating, it is possible to achieve genuinely good practice in developing, delivering and supporting learning. The following are all real examples from published accounts of inspection or best practice in PCE, which have been selected to represent best practice across the sector.

Local Education Authority (LEA) family learning programme

Family learning programmes are organised for parents and children to learn together, often to help families develop family literacy. This LEA went through a series of stages when setting up its family learning programme, which helped to make sure it worked. Running throughout the programme is the involvement of all key people, effective communication, making changes based on feedback, and providing effective support for students and learning. By taking this approach it was possible to:

- agree which courses would be put on, based on detailed discussions with schools and families;
- run lively and engaging information and taster sessions to include family suggestions for developing a suitable course;
- induct participants with maximum support;
- record learning and achievement on an ongoing and simple basis throughout the courses;
- provide opportunities for progression and achieving of qualifications.

Many of the students involved in this programme have grown considerably in confidence, gained recognised qualifications and progressed to further learning.

Improving retention in hairdressing training

A large college operates hairdressing apprenticeships, which have recruited between 110 and 180 trainees each year over the last three years. Training takes place at the college, in the workplace, at outreach ICT centres, and participants make some use of home study. The leaving rate from these programmes has been high, due to low trainee motivation caused primarily by low wages, a sense of limited progress with the training and few opportunities to make an impact in the workplace. A project team was set up to work with new apprentices, employers and the teachers involved, and first investigated more thoroughly the reasons for low retention, then strategies to change the situation. A wide range of employers, trainees and staff were involved and the project:

- developed a more flexible approach to the training, with improved linkages between the workplace, the college and the staff involved;
- changed the curriculum to promote achievement at an early stage and to add motivation for trainees;
- provided supportive trainee reviews more frequently, with regular employer involvement;
- used trainee, staff and employer feedback actively in developing the programme;
- actively celebrated success and publicised salon names.

The project contributed to a significant improvement in retention (31 per cent) and committed and sustained support from employers for the approaches used. In addition, there have been a number of unexpected outcomes including stronger working relationships among all participants, smoother running of the college-based training and more use of support services by apprentices.

Teaching master classes

Five further education colleges, two adult and community learning providers and two private training organisations collaborated to develop an annual training day built around the idea of promoting excellence in teaching. Teachers with an excellent teaching track record (as shown through observations, innovations or excellent achievement and retention) in those organisations were approached. They were invited to a planning day to devise a mixture of sessions or 'master classes' around certain themes and were given free rein on how to approach this within those themes. The resulting programme was made available to all teaching staff from all the organisations concerned, as an 'away day' at a centrally located conference venue. Facilitated discussion groups were interspersed with the master classes to provide a forum for issues raised. As the day progressed, 'scribes' within groups noted results and these, participant evaluations and workshop presenter evaluations formed the basis of a report which was circulated to all attendees.

Results of the day showed that:

- the master class leaders felt valued, enjoyed sharing their experiences and identified areas where they could further improve;
- participants in the day valued the workshops highly, but equally valued an opportunity to network and share views and experiences with others;
- the participating organisations noted increased confidence and motivation among their teaching teams and a localised approach to developing master classes;
- the event gained local and in due course national media coverage;
- other areas which heard about the scheme planned to do something similar.

The people not paper manifesto

These examples in many ways illustrate what this closing section of the chapter is about to say, which is that

bureaucracy and preparing for inspection don't have to be a painful drudge.

The focus throughout the examples above is on people, not on paper. The systems and processes are set up to draw people in, welcome their views and listen to what they say. This information is then compared with other relevant information, some of which is statistical and quantitative, and set in a wider context. Informed decisions on ways forward are made, action taken, and the people involved again in that action. Imagine this as an idealised (though possible) scenario for a 'people not paper' approach to quality assurance.

- You arrive at work and log in to one of the staff computers. Three reminders pop up on your screen. Your second group of the day are due to complete their mid-course online evaluation questionnaire; at midday, you have a course team meeting, where one of your colleagues is doing a mini-presentation on 'using tutorials to boost retention'; tomorrow is a 'feedback half day' which is reserved for all of the course advisory groups to take place across the organisation.

- After a tricky first session, where three of your students were late, you log in to the agenda for the advisory group and add 'student lateness' for the student reps to discuss.

- While your second group are completing their online questionnaire and submitting the results to the centre for evaluation and development, you take a look at an analysis of the results from the last two years, provided by the centre, and update your journal on actions taken. The system tells you your action plan has been updated and your group return for the face-to-face discussion of points they have raised, which is required at the mid-course evaluation stage.

- The presentation at your course team meeting provokes a lively discussion and you go away thinking about trying out some of the things suggested. The course team secretary asks you to countersign the minutes before they're added to the electronic course file.

- At the end of the day you stay for a few minutes to update your paper copy of your scheme of work to build in trying out the new ideas and put it in the departmental admin pigeon hole, so that it can be updated tomorrow.

- You leave for home, tired but upbeat, before 6 pm.

References

Lea, J. (2003) Overview: the organization of post compulsory education, in Lea, J., Hayes, D., Armitage, A., Lomas, L. and Markless, S. *Working in Post Compulsory Education*. Maidenhead: Open University Press

Learning and Skills Council (2003) *Learning and Skills Beacons*. London: LSC

Learning and Skills Development Agency (2004) *Quick Guide to Effective Practice – Inspections*. London: LSDA

Managing your managers

In Chapter 16, when addressing the way power works in organisations, reference was made to 'position power' as the power which comes from a person's formal position in an organisation. The people who hold most position power in organisations are usually (though not always) the managers. This chapter gets inside the nature and role of managers, starting with an explanation of the somewhat negative image of management in PCE. A glimpse into the manager's world follows, and an opportunity to recognise that they are also subject to many and varied pressures. We then reflect on the differences between managing and leading, and suggest there is perhaps too much of the first and not enough of the second in PCE. The chapter concludes with some hints and tips about how you as a teacher can successfully work with and for your managers.

Management of PCE in context

The way management has developed in PCE over the last 20-plus years has been described as the 'new managerialism' (Randle and Bailey 1997a; Lea 2003). To put it simply, managerialism is a term which is used to describe the use of business approaches, systems and practices in the public sector, which were originally more commonplace in the private sector. Managerialism emphasises two key areas, accountability and efficiency, and normally involves:

- ensuring recruitment, retention and achievement of students is paramount;
- balancing efficiency and effectiveness;
- focusing key activity on the organisation rather than on the individuals within it;
- flexibility of teaching staff within the needs of the organisation;
- organising the resources for education on the basis of market demand and value for money;

- basing quality assurance on outputs and performance indicators;
- placing control of the organisation and its activities in the hands of the managers.

(adapted from Randle and Brady 1997b)

A number of influential writers have argued that new managerialism has brought with it negative consequences for teachers, students and organisations, including:

- a reduction in the level of consultation with staff and the concentration of power at the centre of an organisation in the hands of a few (Lomas 2003);
- an emphasis on enterprise, income generation, local competition and survival in the marketplace at the expense of more general educational goals (Watson and Crossley 2001);
- dilution of the authority and autonomy of professionals and its replacement by the power of managers to establish agendas and to determine work patterns (Simkins and Lumby 2002).

Who are the managers?

Once again, the diversity of PCE presents us with a problem. In a small organisation, everyone may to some degree have a management responsibility. Even in a large FE college, many roles involve taking responsibility in a management sense. A section head in a large college may manage a greater budget than the whole of an adult and community education department at a local authority. Common management roles which exist in PCE are:

- principal – the most commonly used name for the head of a further education college (and at times other PCE organisations);
- senior manager – usually part of a small group who comprise the executive management of any organisation, such as directors or finance managers;
- head of department/faculty – those with overall responsibility for a curriculum area or group of related curriculum areas, e.g. health and social care, humanities, construction;
- cross-institutional manager – those who work across an organisation with a developmental, service or organisational role such as head of learning support, management information services, quality management, learning resources;
- middle manager – those who are not part of the senior management team but do undertake management responsibilities.

Even within these roles, there can often be blurring of the boundaries, depending on the size and nature of the organisation. One key factor, which I am not necessarily presenting as negative but which certainly has a major impact, is this:

Many managers in PCE may not come from an educational background and may never have taught at all.

> ### THINKING POINT
>
> **Who are your managers?**
>
> ● Who manages your organisation and what effect does that have on you and your students?
>
> ● How are decisions made and do you have any influence?

What does a manager in PCE do?

These two examples of managers are deliberately from different PCE contexts to illustrate the varied demands of day-to-day management. While very different in many ways, both managers also encounter a surprisingly similar range of challenges.

The company learning centre manager

Marina manages a learning centre in a company with 230 employees. The centre has an open-access computer suite, an office and two classrooms/seminar rooms. In addition to being the learning centre manager, Marina is the union learning champion in the company and manages access to the centre by the local community and local businesses, which is a requirement of the funding which set up the centre. An inspection of the local learning centres is taking place in three months and the self-assessment plan for that visit is due in very soon. The centre's three paid staff are coming to the end of their one-year contracts and at least one will be losing their job unless the centre gets nearer to hitting its annual targets. A major bid for new funding for the next three years, which Marina is writing, is due in next week. The next basic IT course, which Marina is teaching, starts in ten minutes and two of the computers are down. Employees working shifts have been complaining they can't get access to the centre immediately before or after the night shift.

The college principal

David has been in his job for three weeks and has taken over a college with mediocre inspection results for the last two inspections. Improving that situation is one of his key responsibilities. The proposed budget for the next financial year is showing a need for efficiency gains, which will leave little scope for improving the ageing buildings on the college campuses. A new government policy requires all new teaching staff to take an introductory 'survival course' to make sure they can start teaching effectively as quickly as possible, and the teacher trainer who would be teaching this course has just gone off on long-term sickness leave. At his most recent senior management meeting David was relieved to get a positive response from the rest of the executive to his proposals for the future of the college, though the head of curriculum explained that the staffing cuts 'could be tricky' with the union and academic committee involved. David has just heard that his offer for a local house has been accepted, so he will shortly be able to move out of the hotel he has been living in for the past month.

THINKING POINT

Would you want to be a manager?
I have of course exaggerated to some degree to illustrate the point, but these are genuine problems and dilemmas which our managers in PCE face every day.

- How would you respond to the challenges in these examples?

- Could you balance educational and management values to make decisions?

- Would you need to compromise your views and values and how would that make you feel?

- Would you rather leave management to someone else?

Management or leadership?

As you can see from the examples given, much of what managers face involves what is immediate or impending. Management is more than fire fighting and working with the here and now, but at times it can be difficult to move outside of the short term. Examining some of the potential differences between 'managing' and 'leading' helps to understand some of the pressures and to find ways forward. McGrath (2004) produces a useful analysis of 'what managers are concerned with', and 'what leaders are concerned with', drawing on a number of other sources in the field – see Table 19.1.

We are not arguing for either a management only or a leadership only approach. As Glatter (1997: 188) puts it nicely, 'indifferent management can be good enough to secure survival in some contexts, while even talented leadership can fail to prevent closure or amalgamation in others'. Chapter 20 concentrates more on leadership, but we would argue that the key is to be balanced:

A blend of management and leadership should be the goal for PCE.

Table 19.1 Managers and leaders

Managers are concerned with	Leaders are concerned with
The present	The future
Planning and budgeting	Building vision and developing strategy
Monitoring and control	Exercising influence
Providing a sense of order, staying on the right path and doing things right	Providing a sense of purpose and doing the right things
Maintenance of systems and the status quo	Working positively with change
Organisational structure and staffing	Drawing people together and building consensus
Problem solving	Problem seeking
Economy and efficiency	Effectiveness
Staying on course	Making new paths

(adapted from McGrath 2004)

Leading from the middle

How can that blend and balance be best achieved? In her analysis of FE middle managers' roles in strategic decision making, Leader (2004) suggests that

managers can lead from the middle.

This statement is used in relation to middle managers, but is very much about balancing managing and leading. We would argue that management in PCE would benefit by moving away from over-concentration on managing day to day and moving to leading the sector to a more positive future. In simple terms, this is about moving away from management towards leadership. Adopting these key principles could make a significant difference:

- Never lose sight of the key mission of providing inclusive learning opportunities for your students.
- Day-to-day business is important, but there is a tomorrow.
- Inclusive approaches to managing will work.
- Trust the autonomy and capability of middle managers and teachers.
- Devolve leadership.
- A practical, systematic approach to organisation and communication is appreciated by staff.
- A shared vision may be better than your vision.
- You are allowed to be nice and still be a manager.

Managing your managers

This is essentially your strategy for survival in this area. First, don't forget what I have already said repeatedly about the ways you work with your students and your colleagues. You may find it more difficult to be 'actively critical' with your managers, but what you have learnt about group dynamics, personality types and organisations is essential to understand and manage your managers (and for you to use if you become a manager). Follow these guidelines, adapted from Geisler (1999), and you should work well with your managers:

- Know your manager's style – how does he or she prefer to interact with staff? Face-to-face meetings? Memos? Drop-in visits or with an appointment? Do they engage in social communication or is it all business?

- Be sensitive to your manager's current challenges – the more you know about your manager's workload, the better you can work out how and when to add to (or reduce) that workload. This is largely a matter of being aware of what is going on in your organisation, but is also about the bigger picture and simple observation.

- Timing is important – be aware that some times are better than others to approach (or disagree) with your manager, and be able to pick your moments.

- Know your manager's values – if you can (and wish to) connect with your manager's values, this could increase the prospects of the manager being on your side. Be prepared for clashes of values and think carefully about how to work with that.

- Communicate positively – don't forget what I have described previously as 'active calmness . . . which is a combination of relaxed self-awareness and positive thinking'. Be prepared to have ideas and actions challenged and think through in advance how to respond to that challenge.

- Follow up and follow through – don't forget that you are by no means all that a manager has to deal with. If you need to remind them, provide more information, or indeed give support in any way, make sure you do.

Now be brave and try it out!

References

Geisler, J. (1999) *Managing Your Manager: Addressing Your Important Issues*. St. Petersburg, Florida: Poynter Institute

Glatter, R. (1997) Context and capability in educational management. *Educational Management & Administration* 25 (2) 181–192

Lea J. (2003) Overview: the organization of post compulsory education, in Lea, J., Hayes, D., Armitage, A., Lomas, L. and Markless, S. *Working in Post Compulsory Education.* Maidenhead: Open University Press

Leader, G. (2004) Further education middle managers: their contribution to the strategic decision-making process. *Educational Management Administration & Leadership* 32 (1) 67–79

Lomas, L. (2003) Accountability and effectiveness in post-compulsory education, in Lea, J., Hayes, D., Armitage, A., Lomas, L. and Markless, S. *Working in Post Compulsory Education.* Maidenhead: Open University Press

McGrath, J. (2004) Management and leadership in post-compulsory education, in Coles, A. (ed.) *Teaching in Post-Compulsory Education. Policy, Practice and Values.* London: David Fulton Publishers

Randle, K. and Brady, N. (1997a) Further Education and the New Managerialism. *Journal of Further and Higher Education* 21 (2) 229–239

Randle, K. and Brady, N. (1997b) Managerialism and professionalism in the 'Cinderella service'. *Journal of Vocational Education and Training* 49 (1) 121–139

Simkins, T. and Lumby, J. (2002) Cultural transformation in further education? Mapping the debate. *Research on Post-Compulsory Education* 7 (1) 9–25

Watson, G. and Crossley, M. (2001) Beyond the rational – the strategic management process, cultural change and post-incorporation further education. *Educational Management and Administration* 29 (1) 113–125

PART 6

Moving towards mastery

Developing leadership skills

In the last chapter of Part 5 we considered some general aspects of management and leadership and a number of strategies and principles you could use to understand and manage your managers. This chapter begins with a more detailed consideration of different types of leadership in PCE, introducing four models which are relevant. It continues by providing the 'take me to your leader checklist' for you to assess your leadership capability across the four key areas of leading yourself, leading your students, leading other people and leading across organisations. The chapter closes with examples of successful leadership in PCE by showcasing management which has been effective in the real world.

Leadership in PCE today

There are four types of leadership which are particularly relevant to PCE and they have been defined in recent international comparative research as follows.

Transactional leadership

> Transactional leadership is based upon legitimate authority or positional power within an organisational structure. The emphasis is on the clarification of goals and objectives, work tasks and outcomes, organisational rewards and punishments. Transactional leadership requires mutually dependent interpersonal interactions between leaders and members. (LSDA 2003: 5)

This is a leadership style where you are needed by your leaders to carry out defined tasks and goals. If the outcomes of those tasks and goals meet what the leadership needs, you are likely to get a reward. If not, you are likely to be punished. The rewards are expected to provide motivation and the punishment a means of correcting incorrect behaviour. Power within the organisation is concentrated in the hands of a small number of people.

Transformational leadership

> Transformational leadership engenders high levels of motivation and commitment among followers/members. The emphasis is on generating a vision for the organisation and the abilities of leaders to appeal to the 'higher' ideals and values of followers/members in order to achieve high performance, high commitment and high inclusion to an organisation or system. Often associated with charismatic leadership and with organisational change, this form of leadership 'transforms' employees to pursue organisational goals over self-interest.　　　　　　　　　(LSDA 2003: 6)

This is a leadership style where you are motivated to work for the benefit of the organisation and its students rather than for yourself, and where goals and efforts are shared across the whole staff team. Rewards are associated with achieving successful transformation and being a positive part of that change. Power within the organisation is still concentrated within a small group of people and often in the hands of a charismatic leader.

Synergistic leadership

Much theory about leadership, even where it is promoting a democratic approach, has failed 'to include concerns of diversity and (the) female voice' (LSDA 2003: 7). Synergistic leadership is seen as a way of taking more account of diversity issues and the female voice. The role of a synergistic leader shifts from exercising power or inspiring transformation to creating an environment where the full diversity of a workforce is taken account of and the building blocks put in place to make full use of that diversity for the benefit of all concerned.

This leadership style recognises and values expertise, not rank or position, and aims to put everyone in the workforce on an equal footing. Professional development is highly valued and an atmosphere of nurturing and caring is present. Motivation is generated through an emphasis on both individual value and contribution to the organisation-wide community of practice. Leadership does still tend to be the province of a small group of people.

Distributed leadership

> Distributed leadership theory casts leadership beyond individual agency to show how leadership practice is a social process concerned with leadership thinking and action in situ. It focuses on how leadership is distributed . . . concentrating on leadership activity rather than role or position, and on how leadership is stretched over people and situations rather than the individuals' leadership traits.　　　　　(LSDA 2003: 7)

This leadership style sees the organisation as a web of interconnected processes, people and situations, which all combine to achieve its goals. Specialised expertise is recognised and individuals and groups are given responsibility to solve problems and share ideas and efforts. Leadership is seen as everyone's responsibility and the leadership structure is developed to support and sustain that collective motivation. Everyone has leadership responsibility and the group of senior leaders must facilitate the effective carrying of that responsibility.

> ### THINKING POINT
>
> **Transaction, transformation, synergy or distribution?**
> Reflect on your experiences of leading and being led.
>
> - Which of the four leadership styles have you experienced?
> - How did that leadership affect you and the work you were doing?
> - How did it affect others such as students, colleagues, friends and family?
> - Which style of leadership do you prefer and why?

Does leadership affect performance?

There is evidence to suggest leadership can transform organisations, but interestingly, when research is carried out into the effect of leadership on overall performance of an organisation:

> there is little evidence in any sector that leadership directly affects overall performance.
> (LSDA 2003: 29)

If leadership in an organisation isn't appearing to affect performance, we would all be entitled to ask what or who is affecting it? There is a clue in the same LSDA research which I have already made use of when it states:

> the results of an evidence-based study (Bell *et al.* 2003) suggested the impact (of leadership) was indirect and the work of teachers, school organisation and relationships with parents and the wider community were key intermediate factors in school achievement. (LSDA 2003: 29)

This highlights something which points to an essential and often underestimated aspect of PCE and other public-sector organisations. When you are the teacher or one of the other staff working directly with students it is fairly self-evident, but to the leaders in an organisation it is surprising how often it is not recognised. When we consider the degree to which power in many of the leadership models is concentrated in the hands of a few, and the pressures on the leaders themselves to comply in many ways, perhaps it is not surprising. My central message in terms of leadership is very clear:

> **Those who make the most difference to the students are their teachers, their fellow students and their closest friends and family.**

Any approach to leadership which does not recognise and make positive use of that capacity of teachers to make a difference is misguided.

Take me to your leader

Distributed leadership and synergistic leadership are attracting considerable interest at present. They both recognise shared responsibility, problem-solving approaches and individual and team expertise, and emphasise the importance in any public service of the front-line workers. In simple terms, if your teachers are working at full effectiveness with their students in a consistent manner across the organisation, the chances are everyone will be more satisfied and achievement will improve. For this to work and for more people in your teams to develop leadership capability, time and resources need to be invested in leadership development.

Leadership development activities

Don't worry, we are not suggesting you go off to the jungle and build huts or wrestle with giant insects, much as you may want to! These 'take me to your leader' activities are intended to let you think about the leader in you through the use of a self-rating checklist and a group exercise. They reflect a combination of accepted positive leadership models and my vision of the 'reflective professional', which is central to the next chapter. The four key areas of leadership are as follows:

- Leading yourself – this is about the ways in which you understand and work with your strengths and weaknesses; how effectively you communicate overall; how ready you are to take responsibility for your actions; what your approaches are to risk taking, innovation and change; your capacity to plan for the future and develop your capabilities.

- Leading your students – this is about the way you understand, work and communicate with your students; how you develop their capacity to take responsibility for their actions; how you encourage them to innovate, take risks and manage change; how you assist them to develop their capacity to plan and develop towards the future.

- Leading other people – this is about how you understand, work and communicate with other people at all levels of your organisation; how you help them to develop their capacity to take responsibility for their actions; how you work collaboratively with them to innovate, take risks and manage change; how you work with others towards the development of their capacity to plan and develop towards their goals and those of the organisation.

- Leading across organisations – this is about how you can work and communicate across institutional boundaries at all levels; how you contribute to developing a responsible and accountable organisation; how you foster balanced risk taking, innovation and change management; how you create conditions for a forward-looking and responsive organisation to thrive.

Take me to your leader self-assessment

When completing the checklist (Table 20.1) give yourself an honest rating from 1 to 4 for each item. If you feel the rating is different for different situations, complete more than one checklist. The key to the rating is: 1 = no competence; 2 = some competence but need more development; 3 = generally competent in most situations; 4 = competent in all but a few situations.

Table 20.1 Take me to your leader self-assessment

No.	Area	Rating (1–4)			
		1	2	3	4
Gaining the respect of your students, work colleagues, managers and others					
1	being familiar with the educational and professional backgrounds of your students and colleagues				
2	listening actively, consulting widely and being open to the concerns of others				
3	building shared views and goals				
4	treating all others with respect and fairness				
5	working collaboratively to solve problems				
6	encouraging thinking 'outside the box'				
7	arguing positive cases effectively with senior managers and peers				
Developing individuals and groups through direct and indirect day-to-day interactions					
8	developing learning, work and organisational objectives as a shared enterprise				
9	promoting innovative and creative approaches				
10	negotiating access to appropriate people, physical and financial resources to achieve objectives				
11	agreeing and carrying out strategies to monitor and review achievement of the objectives and developing appropriate evaluation tools				

Table 20.1 (continued)

No.	Area	Rating (1–4)			
		1	2	3	4
12	working towards the planned objectives in an organised manner				
13	agreeing and making necessary changes to objectives as needed				
14	building individual and group ownership of the objectives				
Energising performance – supporting others in working to effectively fulfil their potential and complete activities					
15	maintaining clear and positive channels of communication between all parties at all times				
16	helping individual and group expertise bond into a creative working team				
17	promoting, encouraging and celebrating individual and group accomplishments at every stage				
18	pausing for democratic, informal and organised feedback on tasks and activities during their progress to completion and ensuring the results are acted on				
19	building in opportunities for further learning and development as activities progress				
20	promoting and presenting the results of individual and group achievement to internal and external stakeholders and leaders				
Reviewing performance and working with performance problems – ensuring the best possible quality of outcomes from individual and group activity					
21	agreeing a schedule of review activity which enables all participants to contribute				
22	collecting evaluation data, reviewing it with all participants and recording the results				
23	arguing for change and development based on the evidence of evaluations				
24	promoting a 'no blame' approach to solving individual and group performance problems				

Table 20.1 (continued)

No.	Area	Rating (1–4)			
		1	2	3	4
25	involving individuals and groups in supporting others who are encountering performance problems				
26	providing opportunities to openly discuss individual and group differences				
Future visioning – promoting learning, development and strategy which meets current needs and looks beyond the horizon to the future					
27	promoting leading-edge research awareness of developments in individual and group fields of expertise				
28	organising meetings to discuss future strategy and activity				
29	providing incentives for developing shared and accessible banks of physical, people and financial resources				
30	continuing to promote and celebrate success and support those performing less well				

Once you have scored yourself, interpreting the results is easy. There are 30 items in all, making a maximum rating of 120 and a minimum of 30. Overall scores could be interpreted as follows:

0–30   You either misunderstood the questions or need to build your confidence and experience across most areas.

31–70   You are showing some leadership potential and need to develop an action plan based on improving your weakest areas.

71–90   You have sound leadership capability and can plan ahead with some confidence to build further on these results.

91–120 You can feel very pleased at your leadership rating, but don't get complacent as PCE changes very fast.

Whatever your results, think them through and make plans to improve on the areas you didn't score so well on and reinforce the ones you did.

Leadership in the real world

These two examples illustrate positive leadership across an organisation and within a small teaching team.

Adult education in a rural county

A large rural county provides an adult education service operating through a network of local centres, each with considerable autonomy. The range of courses is very wide, but student numbers are declining, as are student retention and achievement. The students who participate in learning are mainly from the sections of society which traditionally participate and these are from a narrow range of social groups. The organisation needs to change its culture to be able to remain viable and to widen the community participation within it. In order to meet this challenge, the management of the service decided to:

- consult widely and fully with staff about a changed vision and focus for the service. Results suggested staff recognised the changes were more in tune with the best traditions of adult education and that a more organisation-wide approach to development and delivery would be most likely to achieve that, even if local centres lost some autonomy;

- set up agreed mechanisms for recording and tracking performance against agreed targets, which reduced course cancellations considerably;

- develop partnerships with a wide range of voluntary organisations and others who had access to the target groups of students and considerable educational experience of their own;

- provide support, guidance and coaching for staff to help clarify roles and responsibilities, share good practice and contribute fully to making the changes work.

This approach to leadership by the organisation makes use of some of the distributed leadership strategies we have already discussed and the adult education service is now much more effectively placed to meet the challenges of the future.

Cross-subject peer review

A medium-sized further education college had recently been inspected and results in two of the curriculum areas had been mediocre. After discussion with all staff concerned, the innovative idea of cross-subject peer review was used to look at ways of improving by:

- creating peer review groups comprising the two problem areas and two others from the college with a positive inspection profile, to link up and work together;

- agreeing clear terms of reference for those groups where all participants were seen as equal and where all curriculum areas shared practice through joint workshops and presentations;

- devolving responsibility to front-line teachers to ensure there was no feeling of blame or guilt but rather a shared goal of helping each other to improve;

- being open to change and listening to others which promoted reflection by all on apparent strengths and weaknesses and shared suggestions for improvement.

The results of this distribution of leadership were positive, with all participating staff developing both a greater critical awareness of their own curriculum area and more understanding of curriculum areas they had had little to do with before that point. Internal observations confirmed improvement in the problem areas and the more successful areas identified and used a number of new aspects of learning technology as suggested to them by their colleagues. The experience radiated positive energy out to other curriculum areas, which then started forming their own cross-subject peer review groups.

References

Bell, L., Bolam, R. and Cubillo, L. (2003) A systematic review of the impact of school leadership and management on student outcomes. *Research Evidence in Education Library*. London: EPPI-Centre, Social Science Research Unit, Institute of Education

Learning and Skills Development Agency (2003) *LSRC Leading Learning Report Series – International comparator contexts*. London: Learning and Skills Research Centre

Becoming a reflective professional

This chapter introduces the idea of the 'reflective professional' in PCE, building on what I have so far described as being 'actively critical' by starting with some reflections on reflection itself. It continues by explaining what I mean by a reflective professional and how you can draw on your own experience to grow as a teacher and as a person. The chapter concludes by promoting the sense of support and shared professionalism which can be gained from joining with others in 'communities of practice'.

From the deep end to being a role model

The 2004 framework document on the future of teacher training in PCE argues that 'we want teachers in the learning and skills sector to become role models for lifelong learning (DfES 2004: 5). The European Commission defines lifelong learning as:

> all learning activity undertaken throughout life, with the aim of improving knowledge, skills and competence, within a personal, civic, social and/or employment-related perspective.   (EC 2001: 9)

Even though this definition has its limitations, it is a reasonable starting point, and the inclusion of learning relating to the 'personal, civic and social' domains is particularly welcome. Just what is involved in teachers becoming role models in this sense? Nesbit, Leach and Foley (2004) write about 'great teachers' and argue that they:

> think strategically and act with commitment. When we watch these teachers we can see, and admire, their grasp of teaching technique. But these teachers have more than skill; they also think and act at a number of levels. Such teachers have a deep understanding of themselves and their students, and of the organisational contexts in which they work. They think 'on their feet', and take a long-term view of their work.
> (Nesbit, Leach and Foley 2004: 74)

We all want to become great teachers don't we?

Critical reflection is an important part of that process.

Through the looking glass – analysing your experience using reflection

We all think or reflect on things. It is one of the most natural parts of every-one's lives. The learning wheel I have used in this book recognises the part reflection plays in learning, and Schon (1983) argued that reflection could help professionals to develop their practice. Schon saw practitioners as encounter-ing many problems, grey areas and uncertainties in their work, and used the evocative phrase 'swampy lowlands' to describe those areas. My own watery metaphor of the deep end presents a similar picture, and teachers in PCE can sometimes be surrounded by 'swampy lowlands' on all sides! Schon (1983) sug-gested professional practice could be developed through a spiral of action and reflection, where the practitioner acts, reflects on the action and plans new action, which is informed by the results of the reflection. The spiral is continu-ous and can be interrupted and incomplete, and the reflection will not always solve problems. It can even cause problems. It does, however, help bring uncer-tainties to the surface and provide a means of looking for solutions. This is the basis of critical reflection.

What is critical reflection?

'Without critical reflection, teaching will remain at best uninformed, and at worst ineffective, prejudiced and constraining' (Hillier 2002: xi). This fits nicely with the world view of this book, which recognises and embraces complexity and uncer-tainty, seeing them both as part of an opportunity to learn and develop. But can reflection really make a difference to what we do as teachers? Hillier (2002: 5) is confident that there are two main reasons for using critical reflection:

- We can question our routine, convenient, everyday practices and ask ourselves about what really does and doesn't work.
- We can challenge some of our deeper social and cultural thoughts, feelings and reactions, or what Hillier (2002: 7) calls our 'taken-for-granted assumptions'.

Consider the following examples.

Death by PowerPoint?

You have developed a really impressive set of PowerPoint slides for two of your courses and have used a data projector regularly in your sessions to show the slides. Every student who is present gets a set of handouts of the slides and you place copies on the intranet so they are available for students outside of class times. When you get student work in for assessment, you are a little disappointed to find that no one seems to make use of what is on the slides and no one ever accesses them on the intranet. They seem to make much more use of the extracts from a TV sitcom which you used to illustrate bad practice.

Group activities rule!

You always include a range of group activities, collaborative tasks and projects in your teaching sessions because you strongly believe your students both work and learn better this way. During the sessions there is almost always a good 'buzz' and the feedback from most students about the approach is positive. The achievement in the groups varies fairly widely and is no better than another class where much more traditional teaching is used.

How could critical reflection make a difference?

Both the examples above show teaching generally appearing to be working and there is not a suggestion here that anything is seriously wrong. Look again at the situation and ask yourself just what 'routine, convenient, everyday practices' and 'taken-for-granted assumptions' are present. Try these challenging questions to get behind the practice and assumptions:

PowerPoint

- When I use PowerPoint in my teaching, what difference does it make and how do I know that?
- Why is the other resource more popular?
- Do I use PowerPoint mainly because I enjoy using it?

Group activities

- Do I choose this style of teaching because I personally prefer it or because it works better with and for my students?
- How would I react if I found out that 60 per cent of each session is taken up by my 'teacher talk', that is my own contributions to the session?
- How do I work with students who are uncomfortable with group work?

Critical reflection is about challenging and testing out what you do as a teacher and being prepared to act on the results.

Using the DATA process

Hillier (2002) makes use of Peters' (1994) DATA process as a means of helping critical reflection, and it is well worth trying out. DATA is a problem-solving approach which stands for **D**escribe, **A**nalyse, **T**heorise and **A**ct. The stages are:

- describe the area of practice which you feel needs improvement or change;
- analyse the factors contributing to the problem area of practice. You should dig deep here and consider the assumptions and underlying beliefs and motives involved;
- theorise possible ways to improve the practice and suggest ways forward;
- act on your theory by trying out the new practice to see how it works.

(adapted from Hillier 2002)

THINKING POINT

Trying out DATA

Think of a problematic area of your teaching. Use the DATA process to ask yourself questions about it. This can be carried out alongside formal evaluation procedures. Here are some suggestions:

- Keeping to time, and covering everything you need in your teaching sessions, is a constant problem. Why?
- You use group activity a lot of the time, but rarely give direct input to a group as a lecture or mini-lecture. Why?
- You rarely use learning technology in your teaching. Why?

Reflect on that area of practice through the DATA process and see how the results work out.

The reflective professional in PCE

What type of professionalism can you aspire to and hope to develop in the current world of PCE? I want you all to be great teachers, in the ways described earlier in the chapter. I believe a reflective professional should:

- work inclusively with their students to assist them towards fulfilment of their life and career goals;
- develop and maintain mastery of their core teaching and specialist expertise;
- be actively critical;
- engage with the wider world of education and its communities of practice;

- work collaboratively with colleagues and students;
- develop and maintain their personal vision;
- use their personal experience and professional development to seek to improve teaching and learning in PCE for the benefit of all involved.

Developing reflective professionals should be a central goal for PCE.

Communities of practice

As you are grappling with the 'swampy lowlands', and even when teaching is calm and relaxed, it is highly likely that another teacher somewhere else is having the same or at least a similar experience. It may be a teacher in the session next door or it may be someone in China. It could be happening now or it may have happened years ago. Much as it's nice to feel you are unique, wouldn't it be helpful if that pool of experience and understanding could in some way be useful for you and for others? A positive approach to making use of our 'shared repertoire of communal resources' (Wenger 1998) is to become involved in communities of practice.

A community of practice is a grouping of teaching professionals with shared interests, values and passions, who interact with each other on an ongoing basis.

The grouping can be small, face to face and local or large, virtual and global, and it has a good chance of success if it follows three key principles:

- Taking part should provide worthwhile experiences and understandings for each individual.
- Taking part should provide worthwhile experiences and understandings for the community as a whole.
- The work of the community of practice may benefit the wider community of PCE.

At its best, a community of practice can be a major support to the idea of developing as a reflective professional because it can highlight a number of factors, including:

- you are not alone . . . there are others who are experiencing the same successes and disasters;
- you can push the frontiers forward . . . others will want to work together on trying out something new;
- reinventing the wheel isn't compulsory . . . if and when it has been done before, we can all make use of accumulated and shared experience;
- peer review of quality . . . reviewing practice by and with your peers can be a powerful way of improving quality.

Getting communities of practice to work

Drawing teachers together is not always helpful and not all groupings would be communities of practice in our terms. If you try to follow these guidelines, however, you will give such a community a reasonable chance of success:

- All members need to know clearly what the grouping is for and be able to develop and renegotiate that purpose, and participation, on an ongoing basis.

- Working together on shared tasks, responsibilities and projects can provide an active focus towards shared learning.

- Critical reflection and techniques such as the DATA process need to be built in to maintain focus, but don't overdo it.

- Where there is a social dimension to the community, this adds value and more fun.

Communities of practice in action

Two real examples of how communities of practice can work now follow.

Research into student support

A regional research network negotiated funding for a project to investigate models of student support in colleges and how that affected retention rates. The network included practitioners from across PCE, including further education and higher education. Individually, the participants had different specialist areas, working contexts and backgrounds, but their shared interest in student support drew them together on this occasion into a community of practice. As the project developed, the benefits of working in this way added considerable value, both to the experience of taking part in the research and to the results for the individuals, the group as a whole and the wider field of student support. Innovative aspects of the project and its benefits included:

- carrying out paired research interviews where interviewers visited their paired partner's institution to carry out interviews;

- peer group reviewing and analysis of data prior to producing a final project report;

- collaborative presentation of results at regional and national conferences.

Specialist online communities

The University of Huddersfield operates a residential summer school as part of its PCE teacher training programme. One of the key aspects of the summer school is for teacher trainees to present seminars in their 'subject family' to their peers. The logistics of organising this are problematic, but the opportunity has been taken to create a specialist online community (SOC) for these summer schools. Learning technology has been used to provide opportunities for summer school participants to:

● post and share personal details and information about the seminar they will present;

● access details about the summer school and book into seminars of their choice;

● participate in online discussions considering questions such as 'what makes an effective subject specialist teacher?';

● evaluate different aspects of the experience.

This community of practice has been successful in various ways:

● Participants have been able to sample e-learning in a supported manner.

● Subject expertise has been promoted across geographical boundaries.

● Improvements have been made based on evaluations received.

● The university has secured national funding to develop the community further.

By now you should consider yourself part of that overall community of practice of teachers in PCE. That alone is a considerable achievement.

References

Department for Education and Skills (2004) *Equipping our Teachers for the Future: Reforming Initial Teacher Training for the Learning and Skills Sector.* London: DfES

European Commission (2001) *Making a European Area of Lifelong Learning a Reality.* Brussels: EC

Hillier, Y. (2002) *Reflective Teaching in Further and Adult Education.* London: Continuum

Nesbit, T., Leach, L. and Foley, G. (2004) Teaching adults, in Foley, G. (ed.) *Dimensions of Learning. Adult Education and Training in a Global Era.* Maidenhead: Open University Press

Peters, J. M. (1994) Instructors as researcher-and-theorists: faculty development in a community college, in Benn, R. and Fieldhouse, R. (eds) *Training and Professional Development in Adult and Community Education.* Exeter: CRCE

Schon, D. (1983) *The Reflective Practitioner – How professionals think in action.* New York: Basic Books

Wenger, E. (1998) *Communities of Practice. Learning as a social system.* Systems Thinker: http://www.co-i-l.com/coil/knowledge-garden/cop/lss.shtml (accessed 4/1/05)

You can get involved in research and professional development

In Chapter 17 we considered opportunities worth taking as a teacher and these were projects, research, creating and externalling. Each of those could in its own way be seen to involve aspects of what would be called 'research'. This chapter starts by considering what research is in PCE and whether there really is a time and place for research when you are so busy with so many other things. I strongly argue that research is not just worth making time for but is essential if teachers and the PCE community are going to move forward to a positive future. Examples of research and where it has made a difference are provided, combined with guidance on the approaches, values and skills needed to carry out meaningful and developmental research. Professional development is then introduced as a means of keeping you in touch with the leading edge of your specialist area and as a way of refreshing your teaching. The chapter closes with an appeal to 'get nerdy' by following and maintaining your research and professional development passions.

What is research?

Many of the debates around research centre on these themes and questions:

- 'The truth is out there.' If you look hard enough you can find it.
- 'Life, the universe and everything' are all full of uncertainty in a rapidly changing world, so can truth really be found?
- Does research have to have an 'impact' to be worth doing?
- Is any research genuinely objective?

Discoveries are being made almost every year which would have been considered impossible only a few years ago. Feelings of uncertainty about research and truth are only to be expected in such an environment. In addition, the changes in and development of PCE over the last three decades has been described as leading to the absence of a 'research focus' and a 'research culture' (Hayes 2003: 155). As Lea (2003: 143) puts it: 'The key research concern here is the increasing difficulty we now all have in claiming there is a Mount Olympus from which we can observe educational reality.' Uncertainty about the purpose and value of research is commonplace and thus it could be perceived by pressured teachers, and their managers, that giving time, resources and priority to research is difficult to justify.

Uncertainty about 'educational reality' does not however mean we shouldn't even try to look for it.

I agree wholeheartedly with the powerful assertion that 'all researchers should seek to advance knowledge and truth' (Hayes 2003: 15). Moving understanding of what we do forward, and investigating and questioning policy, principles and practice, is surely essential for us all.

How, then, can we define research? Drawing on Robson (1998), my definition is:

Principled enquiry to help us gain an understanding of the human world of PCE, which can contribute to new knowledge and understanding, and which can inform change and development.

The benefits of research

When a teacher's time is already full up to the point that 24 hours often isn't enough, wouldn't getting involved in research add to that pressure? In some ways of course that may be the case, as research does take time and effort, but it does at its best offer real rewards, including the following:

- You will develop new insights, ideas, materials and skills which will enhance your teaching.

- Taking time to read and be critical about writing and literature through research (especially struggling through the most pretentious writing you will ever encounter) can be a great way of energising your thinking and actions.

- Research credits on your CV can be extremely helpful.

- You will develop a more leading-edge understanding of your specialist area.

- Your capacity to be 'actively critical' will be improved.

- When the next new initiative is about to be implemented in your organisation, you may well be able to make a strong case for how it should (or shouldn't) be introduced.

Making sense of research – lit from different angles

Research is rarely if ever genuinely objective, which needs to be remembered both when using it and doing it. This can be illustrated with an image from film or TV. If you wish to change how your audience views the subject, changing the lighting can be a powerful and effective method, without changing the subject at all. If, for instance, you light a human face from both sides with diffused, soft light, it normally enhances the natural features of that face. If you light the same face solely with strong, concentrated light from immediately below, perhaps coloured red, it will look completely different. In research terms, if a piece of research is being funded by a government, organisation or company, isn't it at least possible that they will want to see the results 'lit' in a way which will agree with their ideas or will show them in a favourable light? If a researcher is investigating the retention of their students, wouldn't they want the results to be seen in the best light for them? When doing research we need therefore to:

- acknowledge the effect which factors such as opinions, values, circumstances and previous research have on research and the research process;
- take account of those factors when planning, carrying out and writing up research.

Research strategies and skills

If you are going to make the most of opportunities to do research, these are strategies you should adopt and skills you should develop:

- Be clear about what you are trying to find out and why. Devise clear questions you intend to ask which relate to the problem you are looking to solve. This doesn't necessarily mean you will effortlessly advance through the research to clear and useful results, but it will start you off in the right direction.

- Get training. Research skills at one level can be straightforward, but in many ways are sophisticated and complex. Training in skills such as developing research ideas, questions and projects, research methods, data collection and analysis techniques, reviewing literature and disseminating and publishing results should be available via your employer or other local learning providers. Take advantage of that training.

- Get access and permission. In simple terms, when researching anyone or anything you will need on most occasions to get permission of some sort, and to make sure the subjects of your research will be there when you want to research them (access). At its simplest level this will involve asking your students, for example, and at its most complex submitting a proposal to a committee which meets only twice a year. If the subjects aren't there or you haven't got permission, your research will not get very far.

- Choose your research methods carefully. There are many methods available to use in research including interviews, questionnaires and observation. Justify and select appropriate methods.

- Don't forget the ethics. Research is carried out mainly by people on people, so the way in which you carry it out should take account of that fact. As the British Educational Research Association (2004: 4) indicates, this is about reaching 'an ethically acceptable position in which their (researchers') actions are considered justifiable and sound'.

- Treat other research/writing critically. Bearing in mind what I said about research being 'lit from different angles', ask questions of other research (and your own) including: Should I take this research at face value? Do the results stand up to scrutiny? Did the methods seem appropriate?

- Find out where your research fits. There is very little in education which hasn't already had some research done on or about it. Finding out what has been done before is really important, as it can guide and inform your own research. Information skills are very important here, as massive amounts of research are now available electronically.

- Always expect the unexpected. It's surprising how often when doing research things don't work out exactly as planned. Just like the rest of life really! This can range from exciting unexpected outcomes to arriving for a set of interviews and finding no one there. Just be ready for it.

- Be confident about what you have researched and the results. Part of the benefit of doing research is that it builds your confidence about the topic of that research. Be prepared to stand up for that confidence in your role as a teacher. (If you have followed my guidance your research should stand up to scrutiny.)

THINKING POINT

Your research project

Taking account of what we have covered so far in this chapter, think of an area of your teaching work which you consider to be a problem and try to create a research question about it, such as:

Why do my students always want to sit in the same place in the class?

or

What is the current thinking on the benefits or otherwise of using a virtual learning environment?

Planning and carrying out a piece of research which could help you to answer either question could be undertaken by:

- thinking through what topics and issues may come up when trying to answer the question;

- finding out the 'state of knowledge' in this area from existing research;

- considering which methods would help you collect data for the research;

- deciding on when, where and how you could do the research.

Now you've worked through this, go ahead and get researching!

Research making a difference

We would argue that research doesn't always have to have an obvious impact, or to change things or to show clear results as it will still make a contribution in other ways. There are, however, many times when it can make a real difference, as these two examples show.

Reasons for dropping out

During the late 1990s, student drop-out from courses, particularly in further education colleges, was still at a relatively high level. The main means of judging why that was the case was to take the official figures of retention for any course (i.e. 20 started and 15 finished, hence retention of 75 per cent) and to rate them across the organisation. Those figures were then compared with figures from similar courses in different organisations and target figures set for retention for most organisations. If a course did not fare well using those measures, it was seen as reflecting on the quality of the provision and the learning.

Research carried out by Bloomer and Hodkinson (1999) involved interviewing a large number of students about what made them more likely to drop out. The results showed that those reasons were complicated and varied and often involved circumstances which were nothing at all to do with the college or its teaching. The key difference which this research made was not necessarily to dramatically change the way things were done but to shift the emphasis away from counting retention figures and towards providing more effective support for students. For the teacher on the ground it wasn't a huge revelation, but it did contribute to the development of a greater range of support services which they could draw on for the benefit of their students. It added significantly to our understanding of why students drop out, even if it didn't provide a complete solution.

Listening to disabled students

An Adult and Community Learning (ACL) service in a semi-rural area had a recorded disabled population of 19 per cent, but only 6 per cent of current ACL students had declared a disability. The team of tutors, organisers and student representatives wished to both find out what lay behind the figures and work towards increasing that participation figure. They got together as a group, including two of their existing disabled students, to help produce a small research project. A postal survey was carried out of students declaring a disability over the last three years and meetings set up at three centres. The meetings were held as facilitated student-only discussion/focus groups and a wide-ranging discussion about many issues resulted. The results included the following:

- Much information emerged which was used to develop plans for future provision.
- User groups were set up for disabled students.
- Plans to improve access and resources for disabled users could be more effectively prioritised.
- Disabled students felt valued and their confidence improved.
- The service organisers recognised that this approach could be beneficial in other ways such as establishing tutor user groups.

Professional development or 'reflective professionals don't stand still'

The new framework for Initial Teacher Training in PCE (DfES 2004) proposes that professional development (PD) for teachers should be continuous, starting with initial training and continuing throughout the professional life of a teacher. Such an official endorsement of PD is welcome, but just what is professional development?

> **Professional development is the process which helps teachers to develop as practitioners, as students and as part of the community of practice of PCE.**

PD can serve a number of purposes, but at its best it can keep us moving forward as reflective professionals, be energising and promote innovation. It can also help us greatly in assisting us to develop and extend our capacity to work effectively with our students. We are always going to be busy, but we shouldn't stand still, and professional development should be an entitlement for all teachers.

The learning curve – guiding values of professional development

The Staff and Educational Development Association's Professional Development Framework contains a statement of values (SEDA 2003) which I feel could serve PCE well. You can use the set of statements to evaluate PD opportunities and activities you get involved in. Professional development should contribute to:

- an understanding of how people learn – ideas about learning and how people learn are constantly developing so this is an important area for all teachers;
- scholarship, professionalism and ethical practice – combines developing a high level of knowledge and understanding in your specialist teaching area and in your teaching in general with the process of being 'actively critical' and regard for the effect of your work on others. Challenging and complex and undervalued in PCE, but extremely important;
- working in and developing learning communities – contributing to shared practice and developing connections and links with other teachers;
- working effectively with diversity and promoting inclusivity – ensuring individual students and groups of students are taught and supported in ways which assist them fully in the achievement of their learning goals;
- continued reflection on professional practice – part of the critical reflection we have considered previously, combining pausing for thought and questioning those taken-for-granted assumptions;
- the development both of people and educational processes and systems – relating the other elements to the bigger picture and what is happening in the world outside.

> **THINKING POINT**
>
> **Does my professional development match up?**
>
> - List any activities you have undertaken in the last six months which you would consider to be professional development.
> - Using the learning curve values in the previous section, check off how many of them were addressed by that PD.
> - Are there areas which are consistently covered or not covered when you undertake PD?
>
> Well done, you've just completed what may be your first ever professional development record.

Get nerdy!

At times, it is possible for PD to get linked up with appraisal, professional registration and a number of other formal and organisational expectations and requirements. Although this is often an important part of developing as a teacher, and provides accountability for development which may have cost a great deal of time and money, it can at times overlook the fact that learning should be fulfilling and fun. With that in mind I would encourage you all to 'get nerdy'. Most of us have deep interests and passions which we find completely absorbing and interesting. For some it may be the history of the British monarchy, for others restoring vintage cars, for others trekking in Peru and for others music in the 1970s. One thing about these passions is that we cannot be sure that our colleagues, friends and family will share them. Hence terms such as 'anorak', 'geek' and 'nerd'. What they do illustrate however is just how important such passions are in our lives and how powerful getting involved in what are essentially personal learning activities can be. As this book draws to a close, I wish to promote the notion that to 'get nerdy' is a good thing. I would like it to be about teaching and learning, but if not, just think of this:

> **If your students end up as absorbed in what you have to teach them as you have been by getting nerdy, you must now be out of the 'deep end'.**

The 'get nerdy' challenge

This is one of the ultimate tests of a teacher.

- Get together a group of your students, colleagues, friends or family.
- Prepare a short teaching session on any subject which gets you nerdy.
- The aim of the session is to develop a change in the views of the group on your passion.

- Run the session and start by asking the group's current view.

- Ask the same question at the end.

If the views have become more positive you can now call yourself a professional teacher!

References

AskOxford.com (2004) *Definition of 'research'*. London: Oxford University Press (www.askoxford.com) – accessed 4/1/05)

Bloomer, M. and Hodkinson, P. (1999) *College Life: the voice of the learner*. London: FEDA

British Educational Research Association (2004) *Revised Ethical Guidelines for Educational Research*. Southwell, Notts: BERA

Department for Education and Skills (2004) *Equipping our Teachers for the Future: Reforming Initial Teacher Training for the Learning and Skills Sector*. London: DfES

Hayes, D. (2003) The truth about educational research, in Lea, J., Hayes, D., Armitage, A., Lomas, L. and Markless, S. *Working in Post Compulsory Education*. Maidenhead: Open University Press

Hodkinson, P. and Bloomer, M. (2001) Dropping out of further education: complex causes and simplistic policy assumptions. *Research Papers in Education* 16 117–40

Lea, J. (2003) Overview: conducting research in educational settings, in Lea, J., Hayes, D., Armitage, A., Lomas, L. and Markless, S. *Working in Post Compulsory Education*. Maidenhead: Open University Press

Robson, C. (1998) *Real World Research – A Resource for Social Scientists and Practitioner Researchers*. Oxford: Blackwell

SEDA (2003) *SEDA's Professional Development Framework – Support and Recognition for Professional Development*. Birmingham: Staff and Educational Development Association

CHAPTER

23

Future gazing – where and what next?

This chapter closes the book by drawing together several key themes. We first take stock of where PCE is situated now in the overall picture of UK education, and conclude that the early twenty-first century is going to be a momentous time for the sector. We gaze into two possible futures for PCE, one grey and gloomy and one positive and energising, and make a plea for steps to be taken to leave the grey behind and head for the positive. The book closes with a final call to all teachers in PCE to work together towards that more positive future, and the final 'out of the deep end test' just to make sure you are now able to swim confidently off towards the sun setting on the horizon.

Where are we now?

In July 2004, the government's *Five Year Strategy for Children and Learners* was published, which gives a detailed overview of what the future will probably hold for PCE. The strategy has many positive messages and argues for an educational system where:

> The central characteristic of such a new system will be personalisation – so that the system fits to the individual rather than the individual having to fit to the system. This is not a vague liberal notion about letting people have what they want. It is about having a system which will genuinely give high standards for all.   (DfES 2004: foreword)

On 14–19 the strategy continues:

> We need to make sure that whatever choices they (*14–19-year-olds*) make, they are prepared as well as possible for adult life – and in particular, for success in skilled employment, in further learning, and – for those who want it and have the potential – in university.   (p. 68)

On adult learning:

> We need to equip people to be 'employable for life'. Skills are at the heart of this, enabling people to take on new roles, and adapt to new circumstances.   (p. 80)

On those such as teachers who are expected to take this strategy forward:

> The people our whole system depends on – those at the front line – must be given the freedom to shape and reshape the offer to meet different and changing needs.   (Foreword)

Although not convinced by what appears to be an overemphasis on 'personalisation' and 'skills', I would certainly welcome much of what is essentially a positive vision for the future which places PCE at the heart of the education agenda.

Despite such positive statements about the sector and its future, the problems in PCE hit the headlines with regularity. Comments made about the results of two reports from OfSTED in November 2004, entitled 'Why colleges succeed' and 'Why colleges fail', described the results as a 'national disgrace' (Curtis 2004). The results were certainly not excellent, and 12 per cent of colleges across the country which were inspected were described as 'unsatisfactory', even though nearly 90 per cent were at least 'satisfactory' and 55 per cent rated as 'good' or 'outstanding' in terms of their leadership and management. In another article, Kingston (2004) pointed to problems of an increasing pay gap between teachers in PCE and in schools (this has been quoted by the national employers' organisation for further education, the Association of Colleges, as approaching 15 per cent) and a rapidly growing overall turnover of staff across the sector of 16 per cent during one year.

These two perspectives, from the official line of the government to the public and media image, which could be described as 'the vision' and 'the reality', typify the contradictions, challenges and frustrations which are everywhere in PCE. It is a sector which manages to get much of what it does right, while at the same time (and probably in the same organisation) getting much wrong.

Where do we go from here?

Professor David Hicks, in his excellent book *Lessons for the Future* (2002), provides an insightful consideration of the place of the future in our education system. The statements from the *Five Year Strategy* about preparing our students for the future certainly address future goals as an essential aspect of what we all do. Hicks (2002: 14) takes a much broader and, I believe, more genuinely aspirational view of the future when he states:

> The future is an integral part of everyday life. We spend a large part of our time thinking about it. Identifying goals for the future enhances our capacity to work in the present, adds to our motivation and helps give us direction. While on the one hand the future is intangible, it is also of crucial importance. Human existence cannot be conceived without it.

Hicks present a convincing argument for the curriculum to 'ask the question: where are we going and where do we want to go, locally, nationally and globally?' (Hicks 2002: 14).

One of the central purposes of this book is to help you survive the present but not to forget the future.

To conclude our journey, I will ask you to carefully consider some aspects of what the future could hold and encourage you as a teacher to 'promote the knowledge, skills and understanding needed to live responsibly in a multicultural society and an independent world' (Hicks 2002: 128).

Two visions of the future

In some respects, prospects for PCE are problematic and difficult. Many of the pressures we face can appear immovable and difficult to resolve and as we have said, the sector is diverse and in some ways not united. The future could lead in two different directions.

Grey and gloomy

Imagine this start to a working day.

08.00   After some difficulty getting access to the building because of a new security system, you arrive at your desk (in an open-plan shared space with 12 others) as usual and start to check your emails. Only 60 unanswered today, which is quite an improvement on yesterday.

8.30   The 20 most urgent are answered. Over 250 still in the inbox. Join the queue by the photocopier to copy handouts to use in your 9.00 session. It ran out of paper 15 minutes ago and your department has exceeded its monthly limit. Collect your memory stick with all the electronic materials for the day and head for session 1.

9.00   At the start of the advanced diploma session, 10 of your group of 18 students are present. The rest arrive in ones and twos over the next 30 minutes, delayed by the new security system which wouldn't let them in to start with. Your PowerPoint slides crash after the second slide, but no technician is available to sort it out for 40 minutes as they have had their hours reduced as part of the efficiency measures. One of your students manages to sort out the problem, by which time the session has only five minutes left.

10.00   Your students go out into the learning centre to work independently on their assignments and you return to your desk, in an open-plan office with 12 others, to finalise your plan for the next session, when you are being observed by the consultant appointed to pre-inspect your organisation.

10.45   After speaking to the eighth student to come to your desk you manage to complete the plans for the session and arrive only to discover your observer has already been there ten minutes. The session goes really well and the observer rushes off to his next session saying 'see you at the feedback session at 6.00 this evening'. He is doing eight in a day and is expensive to employ, so he is holding feedback sessions at the end of the day, which staff have to attend.

12.00   Start your 30-minute lunch break.

12.25   Eat a bought sandwich and gulp a cold coffee after six interruptions of various kinds to your break.

12.30   Course team meeting with six others. Agenda item one, 'improving retention', takes up all the time and the item you were going to give, 'imaginative uses of PowerPoint', is postponed . . . for the fourth time.

13.30   Meeting with your head of department where he asks 'how's the teacher training course going?' and mentions he's not sure whether there's enough money to renew your short-term contract at the end of the year. You answer that you are really enjoying the course but haven't made the last two sessions, as you have been covering for staff who are sick. You explain you will need to start looking for other work.

Need I continue?!

Although the scenario above is exaggerated, all the elements which make it up are present in PCE today. Things could go in that direction.

Positive and energising

We'll call David Hicks to our assistance again, as he suggests three key questions to ask which can help to develop ideas and plans for the future which can be both personalised and collective.

Where are we now?

On the positive side:

- We work in a sector which has a record of embracing diversity, facing and introducing massive change rapidly, and to a major degree successfully.

- We have opportunities to make positive uses of inclusive approaches, learning technology and a flexible curriculum, for the benefit of all.

- Significant improvements to buildings and facilities have been made, with the prospect of more in the future.
- Opportunities for initial training and professional development are likely to increase significantly in the near future.
- In order to meet the expectations and targets set by government, the workforce needs to grow significantly.

On the negative side:

- Teachers in PCE are paid less and their conditions of employment are worse than those of any other teachers.
- Some serious funding issues in the sector have left many organisations facing an uncertain future.
- A number of serious issues about quality in PCE need to be addressed.

Where do we want to go?

- Towards a better trained and qualified workforce.
- To a situation where PCE is flexible for both the students and the teachers.
- To a situation where teachers are consulted and their views both listened to and acted on, at all levels: local, national and international.
- Towards making use of the capacity of learning technology to connect, administer and facilitate interaction and to genuinely reduce the paper mountain.
- To a rationalisation of our labyrinthine qualifications framework into a clearer, more transparent system.
- Towards a situation with more leadership and less management.
- To the recognition that teachers are people too.

How do we get there?

- Teachers have to be better paid and have their workloads reduced.
- Developing and supporting communities of practice for teachers and communities of learning for students needs to move to centre stage.
- Providers should be funded for more long-term security but expected to meet clear goals and objectives over a longer period.
- Teachers should all be provided with an entitlement to supervision, mentoring, initial training and professional development, and the time and resources to make the most of it.
- Governments and other key stakeholders need to show trust in teachers that they can get it right.

Look into your future
Using the same questions, look into your future and commit yourself to work towards it with enthusiasm.

The 'out of the deep end' test

Given the title of this book, I have to insist on asking you some testing questions at the end to see whether the mission has been worthwhile. The change from being 'in at the deep end' to swimming confidently towards the setting sun may well have been quite a journey and you may not yet be all the way there. If you can answer most of these questions with a positive, I can officially recognise you as now out of the deep end.

- Does the prospect of your next month of work fill you with dread or excitement?
- When you are working with your students, can you handle the majority of situations, both expected and unexpected, which may arise?
- Can you remember a growing group of students for whom you have made a difference?
- Are you regularly involved in research and professional development activities?
- Can you effectively stand up for yourself in contact with managers, peers and others?
- Do you make sure you reflect critically on your work and actively seek to improve it?
- Has your specialist area grown in depth and substance?
- Do you work with others to develop communities of practice?
- Are you proud of your job, yourself and the work you do?

You should be, especially if you remember what I said at the start of the book.

> You may or may not feel that education can change the world, but there is no doubt that at some stage, and if you're both lucky and good at your job, you will often help to change someone else's world and life for the better.

References

Curtis, P. (2004) Colleges branded a national disgrace. *Education Guardian* 29 November (http://education.guardian.co.uk/further/story/0,5500,1362028,00.html – *accessed 4/1/05*)

DfES (2004) *Five Year Strategy for Children and Learners.* London: DfES

Hicks (2002) *Lessons for the Future: The Missing Dimension in Education.* London: Routledge Falmer

Kingston, P. (2004) Out for the count. *Education Guardian* 14 December (http://education.guardian.co.uk/further/story/0,5500,1372822,00.html – accessed 4/1/05)

OfSTED (2004) *Why Colleges Succeed.* London: OfSTED

OfSTED (2004) *Why Colleges Fail.* London: OfSTED

Glossary

Achievement	the learning which students complete, usually in terms of qualifications gained.
Additional learning needs	needs which learners have which are likely to mean they will require extra support to achieve their learning goals. Examples are a disability or a learning difficulty.
Attainment	the achievements and accomplishments of our students.
Awarding body	one of the organisations which offer qualifications for learning providers to use with their students. They include City and Guilds, Edexcel and others.
Basic skills	the term for learning which helps adults improve their literacy, language or numeracy.
Benchmark	a standard against which an item can be judged against other items.
Civil society	a term used to describe the goal of an inclusive, socially cohesive society which recognises and values diversity and works towards achieving a sense of community.
Community of practice	a grouping of professionals with a shared field of interest, who interact with each other as a group.
Curriculum areas	the collection of similar subjects which make up a reasonably discrete area of provision, e.g. business and management.
Differentiation	actively planning learning activity to take account of the differences between students.
Hot desking	the practice of providing staff with a group of desks which they use on a first-come first-served basis. Whoever is in uses whichever desk is available.

Inclusivity	an approach to teaching which takes account of and makes adjustments to include all students at all times.
Induction	a structured period of activities to help new employees to settle in and function effectively during the first stage of a new job.
Initial assessments	tests, tasks or activities which students or potential students work through to assist with matching their learning programme to their needs.
Initial Teacher Training	the mandatory programme of training for a teacher in PCE, which leads to them becoming a qualified teacher.
Intranet	an network of computers, usually within one organisation and used by that organisation.
Learning centre	a location, normally in a local community, where learning opportunities are available to that community, often primarily in computer or online courses.
Learning champion	a worker or volunteer who has an official role in promoting learning in an organisation.
Learning experience	any experience from which learning can take place.
Learning styles and preferences	the different ways in which a particular individual may prefer to learn, such as through 'hands-on' or 'visual' approaches.
Needs analyses	a variety of approaches, procedures and activities which can be used to identify particular learning or other needs.
Online learning	learning which takes place using the Internet and other forms of electronic communication.
Open access	courses or centres where students or potential students can drop in or book in at times when they wish to learn.
Profiling	gathering information about aspects of a person to help understand them better.
Retention	keeping the amount of drop-out from your courses to an absolute minimum.
Risk assessment	a procedure for checking the hazards in your teaching spaces and considering the risk of accidents taking place.
Scheme of work	a detailed outline of a learning programme including objectives, content, resources, learning activity, assessment and evaluation, and details of inclusive approaches and differentiation.

Specification document	the full details of a qualification including detailed content, assessment, quality assurance and centre information.
Tutorial	time when a teacher works directly with one or more students to discuss and review aspects of their learning or related matters.
Virtual learning environment	a collection of information, learning content, tasks and activities contained in a specially designed electronic environment, within which staff and student access and use can be automatically tracked.

Index

14–19
  case studies 23, 52–4
  behaviour of students 23, 92
  curriculum 48–51
  future of 49–51
  provision 11, 12, 48–54
  strategy 181
  Tomlinson Report 49
access for all 41–7
Access to Higher Education 15
achievement
  student 18–19, 22, 42, 44–5, 49–50,
    52–4, 90–92
  teacher 18–19, 22–3, 63, 158
  using target setting 83–6
active calmness 116, 153
actively critical, being 39–40, 63, 69,
    117, 134, 153, 165, 178
Advanced Vocational Certificate in
    Education 15, 115
Adult and Community Learning (ACL)
    11, 12, 22, 44–5, 106, 134, 144,
    146, 163
Adult Learning Inspectorate (ALI) 18
A-Level 49, 52
Assessment
  of students 18–19, 35–8, 94, 102,
    141
  in 14–19 programmes 49

  of personality traits 111
  of risks 51, 94
  of skills for life 46
  target setting 83–6
ASSURE model of planning 35–7
autonomy 53, 57, 92, 138, 149, 152

behaviour
  challenging 23, 32, 51–2, 89–96
Bloomer, M. 25, 176
British Educational Research
    Association (BERA) 175
bureaucracy, managing 28–9, 60–61,
    141–7

challenging behaviour
  definition 89
  examples 95–6
  key actions for teacher and others
    94–5
  managing 23, 32, 51–2, 89–96
  types of 92–3
change
  agent 60
  choices for 127
  diary 9
  direct and indirect 8
  in PCE 7–9, 60–64, 162, 173
  in the twenty-first century 7, 123

change (*cont.*)
  managing 7–9, 60–64, 123–5, 135, 157–60
  pace of 8, 55, 135, 162, 173
  through learning 3, 21, 56, 80, 133, 186
classroom
  the future of 24–6
  layout 24
  management 24–26, 51–2
  observation 144
  without walls 25
collaboration 39, 64, 100
Common Inspection Framework (CIF) 18–20
community of practice 67, 77, 157, 169–71, 177
computer – *see learning technology*
conflict
  constructive conflict management 120–22
  co-operative (win/win) 120–21
  definition 120
  explosive 120
  managing 120–22, 134
  situations 121
  understanding 120–22
Costa, P.T. 109
Covey, S. 118–19
Crawley, Janice 84
Crawley, John 120
creating 137
critical reflection 166–7

DATA process, the 168
deep end 2, 9, 28, 29, 62, 132, 165, 166, 179, 186
Department for Education and Skills (DfES) 10, 11, 16, 41, 43, 44–5, 49, 78, 82, 165, 177, 181
distributed leadership 157–8, 163–4

diversity
  and inclusive learning 80–82
  and widening participation 83
  of sector 10, 11, 12–15, 74–5, 106
  of staff 106–9
  student 16, 31, 80–88
'don't panic' approach 29–31

Egan, G. 86
e-learning
  and the wheel of learning 103
  definition 97–8
  enthusiast or sceptic quiz 98–9
  golden rules 101
  in your organisation 125
  positive examples 101–103
  putting the learning into 97–104, 134
  what works with 100
  in planning 37
  of conflict situations 120–21
  through critical reflection 166–8
experience, learning from 3, 17, 20–24, 45–6
experimenting 20–24
externalling 137

five factor model of personality 109–113
Fullen, M. 62–3
further education
  colleges 10, 12–14, 52, 53, 67, 74, 106, 134, 145, 150, 163–4
Further Education National Training Organisation (FENTO) 4, 66, 67, 69, 139
future
  decisions about yours 135–7
  gazing 132, 181–7
  of 14–19 education 50
  of the classroom 24–5
  of the knowledge society 55–6

Gagne, R. 35, 78
'get engaged' 83
'get inducted' guide 28–31
'get mentored' checklist 69–70
'get nerdy' 179–80
General Certificate in Education
    (GCSE) 15, 51
government 19, 48, 49, 98, 181
group
    dynamics 90–92, 109
    management 90–92
    personality traits and 108–13

Handy, C. 9, 20, 21, 124
helping skills 86–7
Hicks, D. 182–4
Hillier, Y. 166, 168
Hodkinson, P. 176
Hoyle, E. 139

inclusive learning
    and diversity 80–82
    defining 80–2
    developing teaching for 81–2
induction
    action plan 31
    official 30–31
    teacher 28–31
    unofficial 31
information
    overload 56
    rich but content poor 55
information skills 55–9
    avoiding 'information overload'
        56
    defining 57
    developing yours and your students'
        57, 58, 59
    in understanding the knowledge
        society 57
    supporting learning 57

Inspection
    and teaching 141–7
    Common Inspection Framework
        (CIF) 18–20
    'people not paper' manifesto 146–7
    preparing for 20
    things can only get better 142

James, D. 25

Kolb, D. 3, 20

language see Skills for Life
leadership
    and personality traits 109–11
    development 159–162
    from the middle 152
    in groups 90–92
    in PCE 151–2, 162–3
    or management? 151–2
    skills, developing 156–64
    types of 156–158
learning
    conditions of 35
    cycle or spiral 20, 166
    from experience 3, 17–24, 45–6
    objectives 36, 37–8
    inclusive 42, 80–82
    organisation 123–130, 134
    personal theory 21
    positive and negative 17
    principles 17–26
    resources 36, 59, 101–3, 107–8
    sites 24–26, 106
    starting points 17
    styles 36, 52
    technology 25, 53, 55–9, 70, 97–104,
        125, 147, 171
    trends in 15–16
    transformation through 3, 41
    wheel of 20–24, 103, 141

Learning and Skills Development
Agency (LSDA) 83, 142, 156–8
learning organisation
definition 123
is yours one? 124–5
learning sites 24–26
learning styles 36, 52
learning technology
as a tool 99–100
and communities of practice 171
definition 97–8
examples of e-learning activity 101–3
in 14–19 53
in mentoring 70
in your organisation 125, 147
teaching with 25, 55–9, 99–103
what works? 100
lifelong learning 56, 165
literacy see *Skills for Life*

making a difference 60, 62, 176–7
management
classroom 24–26, 51–2
middle 149
of behaviour 32, 51–2, 89–96
of time 118–9
or leadership? 151–2
roles in PCE 149–50
manager, managing yours 121, 148–54
managerialism 148
managing
change 7–9, 55, 60–64, 123–5, 135,
157–60
conflict 120–22, 134
learning 5, 12, 24, 35, 51, 57, 58, 76,
83, 101, 143, 153, 166, 174–5, 179
paper, people and pressure 114–18
time 118–19
your managers 121–2, 148–54
Maslow, A.
hierarchy of needs 33–4

mastery 63–4, 76, 132, 155, 168
McRae, P.R. 109
mentor
characteristics of 66, 69–70
mentoring
definition 65–7
examples of in practice 67–9
expectations and entitlements 66
for individuals 66
for mentees 69
'get mentored' checklist 69–70
in organisations 66, 67, 69–70,
134
online mentoring 70–71
training for mentors 69–70
Moser report 41
motivation
in learning 31–5
student 31–5
teacher 32, 133

National Vocational Qualification
(NVQ) 12, 14, 49, 52, 68
numeracy *see Skills for Life*

objectives, SMART 37–8
observation
of your students 32
of your teaching 144
Office for Standards in Education
(OfSTED) 18, 65, 75, 182
'official version' of teaching 18–19
organisation
culture of 125–7, 163
effective teamwork in 111–12
information about your 31
learning 123–130, 134
mentoring in 65–71
Organisation for Economic Co-
Operation and Development
(OECD) 48

paper pressure, people pressure and personal pressure 114–118, 141
participation
    widening 15–16, 48, 82–3
peer
    networking 31, 62–4, 134
    review, cross subject 163–4
    support 30, 62–4, 134, 169–71
persistent questioning 63
personality traits
    and teamwork 110, 111
    colleagues and 108–113
    five factor model 109–113
    impact in the workplace of 109–113
personal vision, building 62
planning
    ASSURE model of 35–7
    for 14–19, 51–2
    plan B 36, 101
    SMART objectives 37–8
    syllabus 38
    for e-learning 100–101
positive change management 60–64
Post Compulsory Education
    definition of 10–12
    future of 181–7
    management in 148–54
    nature of 10–12, 28–9, 60, 74, 106–8, 183–4
    roles and jobs in 106–8
    size of 10–12
    world of 5, 18, 28, 41, 48, 55, 65, 69, 82, 97, 106, 109, 114, 123, 128, 134, 141, 148, 156, 162, 165, 168, 172, 175, 181
power
    of learning 3
    and influence 128–30
    in organisations 128–30
    types of 128–9
    understanding 128–30, 134

practical teaching 5, 15, 31, 51, 77, 81, 86–7, 90–92, 144, 166–7, 176, 179
pressure, managing 114–18, 141–2
prospects, possibilities and opportunities 134–7
principles of learning 17–24
professional
    capable 139
    definition 138
    extended 139–40
    reflective see *reflective professional*
professional development 177–9
    as an entitlement for teachers 177
    definition 177
    framework and guiding values 178
    record 178
professionalism
    characteristics of 138–9
    pathway to new 139, 168–9
projects 136
putting it over 77–8

quality improvement which works 144–6

reflection 20–24, 45, 166–7
reality check 132–40
reflective professional 5, 9, 17, 20, 39–40, 45–6, 56, 60, 62, 75, 80, 83, 98, 111, 116, 122, 127, 132, 135, 138, 146, 152, 159, 165–71, 173, 177
research 136–7, 172–80
    benefits of 173
    definition 172–3
    making sense of 174
    making a difference 176–7
    strategies and skills 174–5
Rogers, C. 86, 116, 135

Schon, D. 63, 166
Senge, P. 123
Skills for Life 13, 41–7
  and e-learning 100
  curriculum 41–7
  including in your teaching 44
  literacy, language and numeracy
    (LLN) 41–7
  Moser report 41
  teaching tips 46–7
  your LLN profile 45–6
social exclusion, reducing 42, 48
specialist subject see *subject
  specialism*
Staff and Educational Development
  Association 178
standards
  induction 29
  national 4
  raising 49
  teaching 4
starting points
  teaching and learning 17–26
strategy for survival 5
  ask those questions! 20
  balancing the group dynamic 92
  becoming an extended professional
    140
  be positive 117
  bin it! 118
  build those skills 46
  calm down 116–7
  choices for change 127
  free to learn 93–4
  get a mentor! 70
  getting communities of practice to
    work 170
  learning experiences 18
  look into your future 186
  making the most of learning sites 26
  manage change positively 62

  one minute listening 87
  picking your dream team 113
  planning ahead for PD 179
  power to the people 129–30
  preparing for inspection 143
  reloading the matrix 119
  riding the waves of change 9
  settling in quiz 30–31
  stand up but share the burden 134
  stay on the wheel of learning 24
  what all teachers should know
    about motivation 34–35
  what can I do about it? 43
  where are you now as a subjects
    specialist? 77
student
  autonomy 53
  body of in PCE 15–16
  diversity 16, 31, 80–88
  case studies, Skills for Life 44–5
  examples and the wheel of learning
    22–3
  information skills of 57–9
  leadership of 159–62
  motivation 31–5, 159
  support 106–7
  working with 31–5
subject specialism
  characteristics of 77
  developing 74–9, 134
  defining 74–6
  groupings of 75–6
  putting it over 77–8
support
  administrative 1–8
  learners 22, 23, 93, 106–7
  literacy, language and numeracy
    42
  networks 67, 77, 157, 169–71, 177
  services 106–7
  technical 108

survival
  skills 4
  strategies, *see strategies for survival*
synergistic leadership 157–8

'take me to your leader' self assessment 160–2
'taken for granted assumptions', challenging 166–7
targets
  hitting the targets, missing the point 84
  meeting 13, 83–4
  setting 42, 83–6
task analysis 77–8
teacher
  and leadership 159–62
  and learning technology 97–104
  and the wheel of learning 22–4, 39
  and mentoring 64–71
  as organiser and administrator 141–2
  career opportunities 135–7
  effectiveness 18–19, 30–31, 62–3, 67–71, 143, 146, 159
  examples of 12–15, 67–9
  great 165–6, 168
  induction 28–31
  'key purpose' 4
  making a difference 158
  new 29, 30–31, 62, 77
Teacher Training Agency (TTA) 29
teaching
  14–19 51–4
  and mentoring 64–71
  and the knowledge society 56–7
  as a moral profession 60
  effectiveness 18–19, 76, 77, 86, 133, 173, 177–8
  experience 12–15

groups 90–92
for inclusion 80–82
methods 36, 44–5, 47, 52–4
promoting excellence in 146
relevance of Maslow's Hierarchy to 34
resources 24, 36, 52–4, 59
skills for life 41–7
using learning technology 97–104
using target setting 83–86
your specialist subject 74–9
teaching and learning
  in the knowledge society 55–9
  starting points 17–26
  working with the wheel of learning 22–4
team
  building 133
  definition 112
  dream team checklist 112–3
  teamwork 111–113
theorising 20–24
thinking points 5
  are you listening? 87
  avoiding explosions 122
  becoming an extended professional 140
  being Tomlinson 50
  could online mentoring work for you? 71
  cup of tea 78
  deep end reality check 133–4
  does my professional development match up? 178
  enthusiast or sceptic quiz 98–9
  good news and bad news 17
  how ASSUREd or SMART are you? 38
  how big is the challenge? 43
  is yours a learning organisation? 124–5

thinking points (*cont.*)
journeys on the wheel of learning 24
journey to change city 61
look into your future 186
mentor or dementor? 66
not the teacher 108
prove it! 142
recognising the three Ps 116
settling in quiz 30–31
storming or performing? 91
the five factor quiz 111
the tortoise and the hare 59
the 'walk-about-audit' 126–7
'three Ps' of pressure 114–18
transaction, transformation, synergy
    or distribution? 158
trying out DATA 168
what all teachers should know
    about motivation 34–5
what behaviour challenges you? 93
what do you think makes a
    professional teacher? 138
what's yours like? 15
where are you now as a subjects
    specialist? 77

who's got the power? 129
would you want to be a manager?
    151
your individual LLN profile 46
your learning sites 25
your own change diary 9
your research project 175–6
time management matrix 118–19
Tomlinson, M. 49–50
transactional leadership 156–8
transformational leadership 157–8
transformation through learning 3, 41,
    80
Tuckman, B.W. 90, 91

values 56
vision of the book 6

wheel of learning 20–24, 35, 103,
    141
widening participation
    scenarios 82–3
    to learning 15–16, 82–3
workplace learning 11, 53–4, 68–9,
    145–6, 150